P9-EDQ-452

Old Age
Is Contagious

but you don't have to catch it!

LEE PUBLISHING
1354 Miller Place
Los Angeles, California 90069

Old Age Is Contagious

©1985 by Eve Blake

All rights reserved. No part of this book may be reproduced without the express written permission of the copyright holder. Permission is hereby granted to legitimate literary reviewers to reproduce excerpts in their reviews.

International Standard Book Number: 0-939171-007

Library of Congress Catalogue Card Number: 85-060307

Printed in the United States of America

Second printing 1986 by
Third printing 1989 by
Fourth printing 1993

Lee Publishing
1354 Miller Place
Los Angeles, California 90069

For Dick,
Without whose caring
this book would
not have been written.

Foreword

The Irish playwright, Sean O'Casey, says, "We must begin early to absorb life so that when we grow old we may be filled with its colors, thoughts and sounds ... If we don't, then the old seek relaxation in being a misery to themselves and a damned nuisance to others."

For those who, like myself, are determined to avoid at all costs becoming "a misery to themselves and a damned nuisance to others," this book is written.

And it is dedicated to the proposition that all men are created equal—equal to kicking the habit of old age, if they're willing to kick with sufficient ferocity and with sufficient tenacity.

1.

"God, I hate getting old!"

The vehemence in the voice made me turn my head. The words had been flung out by a woman seated next to me at the lunch counter. She was a pleasant-looking woman of perhaps fifty-five who was studying the menu.

"Can't read a menu at all any more without glasses." She yanked her glasses out of her purse. "Blind as the proverbial bat. Isn't it horrendous to get old?"

I shrugged. "I have a niece who's just 19 and she can't see her hand in front of her face without glasses. What do you mean by old?"

"Well," she paused for a moment, then spread her hands in an impatient gesture, "old ... that murderous monster that sinks his fangs into everyone with the years!"

"You know, it's quite interesting—Mr. Webster's definition of the word 'old'. Have you, by any chance, ever looked it up?"

She shook her head vigorously. "No. I don't want anything to do with the word!" She lifted a glass of water to her lips, then, with the glass in mid-air, she turned to me. "What did he say?"

I smiled. "Well, he defines old as 'outgrown useful-ness—belonging to the past—shabby—stale.' Would you be-lieve—not a single syllable about needing glasses to read the menu. Really."

She laughed. Then her face took on a thoughtful look. "That *is* interesting."

"Puts an entirely different complexion on the word, doesn't it?"

And it does, you know, if you think of it that way, if you ponder the accurate definition of the word 'old', "Outgrown

1

usefulness—belonging to the past—shabby—stale."

Of course, when I quote this definition to some people—and, parenthetically,, I must say that I'm exceedingly fond of quoting this definition by my good friend, Mr. Webster—they say to me, "But even so, when I look at the calendar, it informs me that a certain number of years have passed. You can't get away from that!"

Certainly years have passed, according to the calendar. But how does that tie in the word 'old'? What has the calendar to do with age when even medical doctors agree that aging is a completely individual process; that physical decline takes place in different people at different times of life and that their degree of vigor is widely variable.

Doctors divide age into two separate categories; chronological age, the actual number of years a person has lived, and physiological age, meaning how old the body is in terms of deterioration. Since this is so, two people who have a chronological age of 65 years may have a widely varying physiological age, the one as low as 50 and the other as high as 80. So at 65 one of the two is definitely old and the other is definitely not.

I happen to know personally two men who are the same age, according to the calendar. Of one everyone says, "He's an old man," and of the other, "You'd never in the world believe his age. He's absolutely incredible!" That's the only way to be. Incredible! That's the way I've decided I'm going to be. And I have a good sporting chance. Because my grandmother was incredible.

I remember one day calling her and asking if I could drop by to see her. Her answer was, "Darling, I'm so busy. Could you possibly make it another day?" She was 83 at the time. And she was so busy she couldn't find time to see her favorite grandchild!

Then I remember another day when she asked me if I would go out and buy her an English grammar. She said she was very eager to learn to write English. My grandmother was Hungarian and although she'd learned to speak and read English since she had come to America, she'd never learned to write it.

I was curious. "You want to learn to write English—*now?*

Whatever for? You planning to go out and get a secretarial job with General Motors or something?"

"Maybe." She grinned her beautiful grin. "It's not a bad idea."

"All right. Tell me."

"Well," she said, very seriously now, "when I die and go to heaven and meet all those wonderful people up there, I don't want to be embarrassed by not being able to write English."

I said, "But Gram, what makes you think God's an Englishman? He could very well be a Hungarian, you know, and you wouldn't have any use at all for English. All those other people would be the ones embarrassed because they couldn't write Hungarian."

She gave me a small, affectionate shove. "Go—get me the book."

I bought her the book and she learned to write English. At 84.

She died a few years ago. I hope with all my heart that God turned out to be an Englishman and that he's delegated her to scribble her not-quite-perfect English on every available wall in heaven.

In sharp contrast to my grandmother is the mother of a friend of mine. She, too, is 84. But she's sour and senile and—she's old. So you see, the calendar is no authority to consult about your age. How many birthdays you've had has very little to do with how old you are. As Ralph Waldo Emerson says, "We don't count a man's years until he has nothing else left to count."

"But even if I don't consult the calendar," people have argued, "I look in the mirror and I can see that I'm getting old."

How? More wrinkles? Graying hair perhaps? That's a very spurious proof of age when we bear in mind Mr. Webster's definition. Outgrown usefulness, he says, belonging to the past—shabby—stale.

Throw away the calendar as an authority! Turn the mirror to the wall! A much more realistic index of age is Mr. Webster's definition of the word "old."

And, in conjunction with that definition, his definition of the word "young."

3

It's quite amazing, when you turn to Mr. Webster, how often you'll find that a word has a completely different meaning than the one we've constantly and carelessly attached to it.

The word "young" is a perfect case in point. As Webster defines it, young means "to be youthfully fresh in body or mind or feeling." Of course this is most reassuring, particularly if you're a woman and this little jingle happens to hit home:

> *That whistle when I hear it now*
> *Serves only to remind me*
> *That probably a pretty young girl*
> *Is walking right behind me*

Just hang on to Webster's definition at a time like this. Remember he specifies that being young means being youthfully fresh in body—*or* mind—*or* feeling. Certainly Winston Churchill, when he was 70, was not young in body. But he was so young in mind and feeling that he was described in public print—at 70, no less—as a "young man with a bright future."

Winston Churchill, of course, was one of the lucky ones. He probably gave little or no thought to staying young. I would hazard a guess that it was instinctive with him. But I'm afraid it's not always that easy. For most of us it takes a lot of doing.

Alexandre Dumas, the French novelist, for instance, was an extremely alive and active man all of his life and when he was well along in years, a lady came up to him and gushed, "Mr. Dumas, how does it happen that you stay so alive and youthful?" His solemn reply was, "Madame, it doesn't *happen*. I give all my time to it."

Mr. Dumas, it would seem, discovered more than 125 years ago the secret of staying young. This modern-day Ponce de Leon knew then that you have to "give all your time to it." Or certainly a good portion of your time. In any event, you can't expect it just to happen. And in this conclusion I concur wholeheartedly with Alexandre Dumas.

The single big difference between Mr. Dumas' conclusion and mine is that Mr. Dumas gives no specific clues to fending off old age. And in this book I intend to do just that. I'm weary of generalities such as "keep active" and "live in the here and now." They're completely accurate and valid admonitions but exactly how do you go about it?

I believe that there are specific directions on this road to staying young; specific techniques that you can make your own. And this book sets forth some of these techniques. They're simple techniques but they can be exceedingly valuable to those of you who have a strong desire to skinny-dip in the Fountain of Youth.

2.

This project really began with my mother.

She decided one day, some years after my father died, that she no longer wanted to live alone. So it devolved upon me to find a guest home that would suit her.

When I visited the list of guest homes that an agency had provided for me, I was struck with a single overall attitude. In spite of the fact that these were all attractive, comfortable, fairly expensive guest homes, most of the men and women who lived in them just sat and rocked and waited. They waited after breakfast for lunch. They waited after lunch for dinner and after dinner for bedtime. I was not only struck by this attitude—I was utterly appalled by it.

About myself, of course, I was very smug. I thought, "After all, I'm a writer. I've got a good mind. This wretched sort of existence could never, under any circumstances, turn out to be my fate."

Then, to my surprise, I discovered that one of those who sat and rocked had been a rather well-known poetess. She had quite obviously had a fine, creative mind. Another who sat and rocked had been a landscape architect. Obviously he, too, had had a good mind. And the smugness I'd felt slowly drained away. A small prickle of fear ran along my veins. Apparently a good mind was not the whole answer.

What was it then that happened to some people and not to others? What were the reasons behind the fact that some people, despite reasonably good health and enough money, lived out the last quarter of their lives in apathy and boredom while others managed a zestful existence, their days filled with vitality and enthusiasm.

I was totally convinced that somehow there was more involved than blind chance. And I decided to try to track down some answers.

It took more than a year of work, during which time I talked with doctors, psychologists, and nursing home operators. I attended seminars on gerontology; I read medical journals; I pored over papers dealing with the latest research on the process of aging; I studied statistics issued by the government.

And out of this relentless quest began to emerge a validation of the strong feeling I'd had that a stagnant, sterile, miserable old age was not a necessity. Not uncommon certainly. But just as certainly not inevitable.

There was a secret, I concluded, in circumventing it.

That secret was preparation. That secret was, according to Alexandre Dumas, "giving our time" to securing for ourselves alive and productive later years.

Where the financial security of our later years is concerned it's a matter of routine for us to make preparation. We build savings accounts; we invest in stocks, bonds, real estate; our choice of jobs is often influenced by its pension provisions; the self-employed contribute regularly to the Keogh plan. Whatever avenue we choose, it's all with a keen eye to insuring the comfort and ease of our later years.

Our physical health, too, is a matter of deep concern to us. And we make definite preparations to insure that health. We spend time and money on medical checkups; we see to it that our children receive flu inoculations and polio shots; we keep a fierce eye on our weight since overweight has become synonymous with heart attacks; we buy hospitalization insurance to protect ourselves in the event of future medical contingencies. All of these measures we employ quite happily because we've given thought to, and have concern for, our future physical well-being.

And yet, in the one area that is probably the most vital area in our whole lives, we do little, if anything, by way of preparation. Most of us give no thought at all to insuring our emotional well-being. We seem totally barren of concern for our aliveness and happiness in our later years.

Until fairly recently, of course, you could get away with this. It wasn't necessary to devote any thought to the later years. Because there were none. People died young. In the days of the Roman Empire the average life span was 23 years. In 1900 it was still only 47. But the life expectancy has increased steadily until now, according to the statistics issued by the Department of Health, Education and Welfare, American men can expect to live an average of 69.7 years and women 75. For both sexes this is well over 20 years longer than in 1900.

Incidentally, this differential in the length of life between the male and female is not due, as we believed formerly, to tension and overwork on the part of the male. It seems that it's a genetic fact. Research studies into the life of the fly have found that a differential also exists between the male and the female fly. Something to think about. Albeit not very crucial to your life.

However, predictions concerning the longevity of the human being in the next century you will undoubtedly consider crucial. The predictions seem to me almost to boggle the mind. For example, Dr. Albert Sabin, the famous doctor who developed the polio vaccine, claims that people of the 21st century will routinely have a life span of 100 years and, what's even more fabulous, will enjoy lifelong good health.

"Super senior citizens are inevitable," Dr. Sabin said, "because killer diseases like cancer, coronaries and strokes—the leading cause of premature death in people over 65 will soon be eliminated.

"If medical research carries on at its present astonishing rate, these diseases could well be conquered by the end of this century. Then death will come at a time when people are still in good health. They'll go to sleep feeling well and just not wake up in the morning. They'll die because their life spans will have ended. Because some essential part of their 'biological clock' will have run down."

An exciting prospect indeed, even though it sounds somewhat extravagant to us now.

But Dr. Sabin is not alone in his extravagant claims about longevity. The Life Prolongation Research Institute in Madison, Wisconsin, makes claims that sound even wilder. They are engaged in research which they maintain could double the present-day span of life. Headed by the distinguished gerontologist, Dr. Johan Bjorksten, they are working toward enabling the average human to live to be 140 years old.

Archie Bunker, that anti-hero of the television screen, has his own views on the subject of longevity. When asked by his wife, Edith, what he thought of the miraculous strides being made in modern medicine, he replied solemnly, "Edith, you go because He wants you. And *when* He wants you. And He don't want no quack doctors putting new hearts and bellies into you, and keeping you here against His will—'cause it throws Him off His schedule. See?"

For once in his life, oddly enough, our friend Archie is in very distinguished company with his convoluted line of reasoning. For although Dr. Sabin phrases it somewhat more scientifically, he sees eye to eye with Archie. He is deeply concerned with the dangers inherent in "throwing Him off His schedule" by lengthening the life span.

He warns, "Unless future societies take this into account somehow, medical science will only be substituting the misery of loneliness and boredom for the current misery of life shortening disease."

As far back as 1959, Dr. Irving S. Wright, of the New York-Cornell Medical Center, predicted that finding a productive, meaningful and happy life for elderly people whose lives have been prolonged by medical science may be more difficult than finding a cure for cancer.

"Literally millions may soon be existing in a nonproductive, semivegetative state, lonely, frustrated, awaiting an end which has been delayed by scientific advancement," Dr. Wright said.

In the light of these chilling predictions, it would seem to me that preparing for your later years is not just a matter of choice. It seems a matter of crucial importance, a matter of the most urgent necessity. And the price for failing to take those predictions to heart seems so exorbitant I know that I, for one, would happily embrace very drastic measures to avoid any chance of having to pay it.

3.

That fine dramatic actress, Ethel Barrymore, when she had reached the age of 76, said, "A good life is like a good play. It must have a satisfying and exciting third act."

However, any experienced playwright will tell you that when he's tearing his hair out because of difficulty with his third act he usually finds that the source of the trouble is not in the third act. It invariably stems from something that went amiss earlier; there's something dead wrong with the first or the second act. From his experience he knows that if he had laid the proper groundwork his third act would automatically turn out to be a "satisfying and exciting" one.

Along with Miss Barrymore, I feel that exactly the same criteria applies to a life.

The famed Russian author, Dostoevski, sums it up quite simply and succinctly. He has one of his characters say, "One sees yet again that the whole of the second half of human life generally consists of the habits acquired in the first half."

For those of you who feel, as a friend of mine does, that "writers just make things up off the top of their heads," there are some scientific findings that might weigh in with you. Researchers at the Institute of Human Development at Berkeley made a study, one of the longest ever conducted on human beings. It began in the late 1920's and wrapped up in 1969. A continuous flow of social scientists studied the same group of 142 middle class residents through the four decades. And their conclusion was identical with Dostoevski's: OLD AGE MERELY CONTINUED WHAT EARLIER YEARS HAD LAUNCHED. The people who were, for instance, irritable when the study commenced were a great deal more ir-

11

ritable by the time it ended. And the intolerance noted in others in 1928 was found to have increased appreciably in 1969.

I'm sure many of you are familiar with old people who are difficult, crotchety, who are narrow in their outlook, who are prejudiced, or disinterested in everything. However, you've probably made excuses for them. You've tossed around that easy phrase, "Oh well, they're old."

But a little sleuthing into the characters of those old people will invariably result in the discovery, as it did in the Berkeley study, that the traits they're exhibiting now were quite apparent in their earlier years.

A man isn't suddenly transformed into a stubborn old cuss because he's 70. I'm certain that if you check back into that man's character you'll find that he was pigheaded at 40. And the woman who is a domineering old biddy at 70 was almost certainly running everything and everybody at 45.

In line with this thought, the little poem by Lewis Carroll is well worth studying. It's a young man speaking to an old one.

> *"You're old," said the youth,*
> *"and your jaws are too weak*
> *For anything stronger than suet,*
> *Yet you finished the goose,*
> *with the bones and the beak*
> *Pray, how did you manage to do it?"*
> *"In my youth," said the old man,*
> *"I took to the law,*
> *And argued each case with my wife;*
> *And the muscular strength*
> *which it gave to my jaw*
> *Has lasted the rest of my life!"*

The little jingle only underlines the scientists' conclusion: old age doesn't create new habits. It merely emphasizes the old ones. As the saying goes, "The older you become, the more like yourself you become."

It's precisely for that reason that it's so important to pause for stock-taking and self-analysis early in life when there is still time to replace your undesirable traits, if any, with more acceptable ones.

Naturally, to advocate that you change your character drastically would be foolish. You don't have to knock down the walls just to open a small window. If you tend to be on the stubborn side, or even on the domineering side, it's not necessary to do an about face. That's hardly possible, to begin with. But it *is* possible to take stock of yourself. And it's possible—and necessary, however difficult, to be completely honest, completely forthright, in your evaluation. Because awareness enlarges the ability to control. And if you're aware of what you're like, you can at least temper those traits that aren't too engaging so they won't become aggravated and get out of hand and make you a damn nuisance to other people.

Of course if you're lucky, someone you care about—or perhaps someone you *don't* care about will shove you into that self-evaluation.

A wife may shout at her husband, "You are the most inconsiderate man I've ever run into," or, "Why don't you shut up occasionally! No one else in the room can get a word in edgewise when you're around."

Even if one of these remarks is a poisoned arrow straight to your ego, it's an excellent idea to force yourself to listen. And not only to listen, but to consider what's been said carefully and analytically for the kernel of the truth that's probably lurking in it. Particularly if you're between forty and fifty years of age. Because it's just about at that time that the blackbirds of temperament come home to roost.

Of course there's always the possibility that you don't want to change. You may believe it's impossible. Or you may consider it too difficult.

A friend of mine was involved with a man who was, beyond doubt, the most narcissistic character that ever drew breath (which breath he drew only in order to tell you about himself). One day she said to him, without the smallest trace of anger, "You know, you are the most self-involved man I think I've ever known. The world doesn't revolve around you. Honestly it doesn't. Everybody just *isn't* fascinated by each and every detail of your existence."

He listened. Then he said, also without the smallest trace of anger, "Well, I've been that way, I guess, all of my life. I'm

13

fifty-seven now. I can't change."

However, that man was neglecting to take into account a single exhilarating, unalterable fact: a really fervent desire for change is the change half accomplished. Accurately translated, the words, "I can't" mean "I won't." And "I won't" is tantamount to declaring, "I fully intend to let this trait have its head and become exaggerated with the years until I've succeeded in becoming a 'misery to myself and a damn nuisance to others.'"

So you see, you can bank on it—that what ultimately happens to you depends entirely on what you allow to happen to you at this very moment. And I use the word "allow" advisedly. Because it's up to you. It's in your hands. You can allow yourself to become old and withered and boring or you can allow yourself to become mature and ripe and wise.

It's a little like the difference between the way a head of lettuce gets old and the way a redwood tree ages. As it gets old, the lettuce gets wilted and tastes bitter. Whereas the redwood tree never outgrows its beauty and usefulness. When people do mention the fact of its age, they do it admiringly. They look up to it. They make journeys to see it. Rarely does it occur to anyone to think of the redwood tree in terms of being "old." Faced with the choice, there seems small doubt that anyone would hesitate to choose the M.O. of the redwood tree.

Now the question is: how to emulate the redwood tree, how to make sure you don't get old and shabby and wilted. For it's incredibly easy, and without your even being aware of it, to drift into the habits that make you old. And that's exactly what most people do.

However, you don't *have* to do it. That's the exciting part.

These habits can be avoided. If you want. There are only a couple of prerequisites that you need to accomplish that.

First, you need to know the trick involved.

Second, you need to care enough about staying young and vital and alive to be willing to devote time and energy to it right now, wherever your "now" happens to be.

4.

The trick in staying young consists of two parts.

The first part is to be on the lookout for the very earliest signs of aging.

And the second part is to thwart the development of those signs with speed and vigor. This can be done by employing certain definite techniques.

There's a quotation from the Greek—from the writer Ovid, which says, "Withstand the beginnings. The remedy is applied too late when the evil has grown strong through long delay." Otherwise summed up in that well-known American phrase, "Nip it in the bud."

For example, let's begin with the tendency to live in the past that seems to be one of the more common, distinguishing features of age. This particular tendency can be spotted quite easily in its early manifestations.

Often it starts with reminiscing about "the good old days." Now "the good old days" certainly can't be discounted. Very often they *are* "good old days" and they're fun to look back on. But inevitably you'll find that little by little as the years slide by you spend more and more time dwelling on those good old days instead of relishing the present and looking to the future with anticipation. You turn into a "caboose rider," that fellow who's forever in the caboose at the rear end of the train, looking backward, never forward.

I had a neighbor who was an expert caboose rider. He was a judge who, in his younger days, had been a newspaperman. In spite of the fact that he was basically a lovely old man I quickly crossed the street when I caught sight of him heading in my direction. Because almost immediately he would launch into long anecdotes about his early days in the newspaper business. I'm certain he drove away many other people besides me.

That, of course, is a secondary danger attendant on reminiscing about the past. It glazes people over with boredom. So they make a point of avoiding you and the forlorn endproduct is loneliness.

Frequently this tendency to live in the past begins in still another way ... looking back over one's life and regretting. Often people have lost their mates, either through death or divorce, and devote an unconscionable amount of time looking back wistfully, or longingly, or immersed in regret for all sorts of omissions or commissions.

Lodged snugly in the regretting category too are those who feel that they've spent their lives in the wrong job or that they're trapped in the wrong career, all of them indulging freely in that useless little game of "God! If I only had it to do over."

If you're among those who have stumbled into one of those categories, consider the story of Lot's wife in the Bible, who, when she turned to look back, was transformed into a pillar of salt. I feel sure that the writer who wrote that Biblical story was writing symbolically about that very fact that looking back freezes you, keeps you from moving ahead, stops your growth.

In actuality it's a form of suicide. For living entails growth, expansion, burgeoning. And when at any time that growth is stopped, when for any reason that forging ahead comes to a halt, a part of the life force is choked off. And the full flow of life is ended.

Now to head off this tendency to live in the past there's one technique, I believe, that you'll find infallible. If you decide to cultivate it, I guarantee that it will rescue you from getting mired down in the swampy bog of the past.

The technique is never to talk about any event, whether it's good or bad, that occurred more than one year ago. With possibly a single exception: if something helpful has come out of the past that is applicable to a current situation.

Drastic technique? Oh, absolutely. I remember when I advocated it on one occasion, a woman said to me accusingly, "Why, Mrs. Blake, you have just cut out all my conversation!"

Even if cuts out all of your conversation, USE IT. *Particularly* if it cuts out all of your conversation, use it. Because that should alert you to something. You should get the message that, no matter how young or how old you are, already your conversation is top-heavy with the load of the past. Just to make sure, check it out. Ask yourself this question, then give it some honest, painstaking consideration: How much time do I spend thinking and talking about the past?

At the beginning it may be rough sledding for you to abide by the technique without any deviation. It may be annoying as well to have to shut your mouth and chop off some dearly beloved reminiscence in the mid-telling, or have your spouse chop it off for you with a tart reminder.

But just listen to young people when they talk. You'll be struck, I think, by the fact that they employ this technique without even being aware of its existence. They may touch on the past, refer to it perhaps, but ever so briefly. You'll never find them dwelling on it.

Youthful thinking, to me, is summed up in the title of a charming little book by Robert Paul Smith. It's called, "Where were you? Out. What were you doing? Nothing." To some, this may sound like the impudence of a small boy. But to my thinking, it's just that what that little boy did is past, finished, at an end. And he's no longer interested in thinking about it.

Many of you may have noticed how generally true this is of the young. If you've ever had a teenager in the house and have waited to hear details of some shindig that he or she had attended you've undoubtedly run across it. I have a teenage niece who's given me a taste of it on occasion.

Me: "I hear you went to a party last night."

Her: "Uh huh."

Me: (brightly) "Was it fun?"

Her: (indifferently) "Yeah."

Me: "What did you do?"

Her: (with a shrug) "Oh, fooled around."

Me: "How about the boy that took you—what was he like?"

Her: "The pits." Then, "Oh, you've got a new hairdo."

Me: (hopefully) "Like it?"

Her: "Makes you look kinda like a sheep dog ... Well, gotta do my homework."

End of conversation.

Of course I must say they push it a bit far. Sometimes it would be nice if they did expatiate just a little on last night. But last night is the past and, generally speaking, the past holds very little interest for youth. And why should it—when there's the absorbing present and the fascinating future?

It's the sort of thinking we'd do well to emulate. It's the sort of thinking it's incumbent on us to emulate if we're to stay young.

I recall being at a dinner party one night a couple of years ago. It was just after I'd returned from a trip to Japan. When the hostess mentioned this, her husband turned to me and launched into a recital of *his* trip to Japan.

"Oh," I said pleasantly, "when were you there?"

"During the war," he said.

"During the war?" I was slightly taken aback. "You mean—what war?"

"World War II."

With the slightest edge to her voice, the hostess said, "Darling, that was 40 years ago."

He gazed off into the distance with a fond, faraway look. "I know. But it doesn't seem like any time at all." Then he turned to me eagerly, "Wait till I tell you about the time when—"

Sweetly the hostess cut in, "Shall we adjourn to the living room, everyone?"

Whether the hostess' words came at that moment by accident or design I never knew. But in either event, I sent her my blessing.

So if by any chance you should be involved in a conversation and you hear those words: "Let me tell you about the time when—" or "When I was young," or perhaps, "On my first job—" and you suddenly realize that those words are issuing from your mouth, clamp it shut post-haste.

It will pay off in generous dividends. For you'll find that this technique, once you've made it habitual, will be wondrously effective in stripping away that glaringly conspicuous badge of old age—the endless conversation about what's long gone.

5.

There's a nice story about an elderly gentleman who was celebrating his 100th birthday and he was being interviewed by a young newspaper reporter. The reporter thought of all the wonderful innovations that had come about during the old man's lifetime—the automobile, the airplane, the electric light, television—and he said respectfully, "My, sir, you must have seen plenty of changes around here in your time."

And the retort was, "Sure have. And I bin agin every single one of them!"

Naturally most people don't come out with it as boldly as did the old gentleman. But they feel that way nonetheless.

Unfortunately, fixed ideas are an implacable enemy of youth. Even more than stiffening of the joints, this stiffening of one's ideas makes for age. "When I was young, children didn't carry on like this," or, "The world's going to pot these days," or "Times have certainly changed."

Remarks like these are standard procedure for most people. I'm sure you've all heard them many times. Perhaps you've even been the guilty party on occasion. For it's so easy to look on all change as bad and on everything static as good.

But it's as dangerous as it is easy. And it's imperative that you make a valiant effort to resist that first impulse to be "agin it." Instead, consider the possibility that the change could be for good. It could, you know. But even if it's difficult for you to believe that it could, it's vital that you make the attempt.

It's vital because it's so essential to stay flexible in order to stay young.

Flexible of body, of course. With that we're all pretty

familiar. We're bombarded on all sides with the value of golf, yoga, sit-ups, simple bending exercises and now, more recently, aerobic dancing, in maintaining the flexibility of the body.

But of even more importance, and not nearly so well-publicized, is flexibility of mind, of thought. This flexibility of thought is not only important in keeping you young, but there's a side effect. The delicious added bonus is that the more flexible you are as a human being the richer and the more painless you'll find your life to be. You won't be bound up in the anxiety-provoking straitjacket of rigidity. And if, on occasion, you do find yourself wrapped in that straitjacket and events occur that force you out of it, you won't be thrown into a panic. You'll be able to make alternative choices easily and even derive pleasure from them.

As with any other habit, flexibility of mind must be practiced constantly, faithfully, and I have a most practical technique to offer that will lend wings to the doing. If you choose to adopt it, it's practically guaranteed to prevent "rigor mentis" from setting in.

This technique is to do something each day to force yourself to deviate from your regular routine, whatever it may be.

At the onset, it might be somewhat less difficult to make the variations small ones. If, for instance, you're accustomed to taking a bath in the morning, try taking it at night. If you happen to be one of those who say, "Oh, I never take a shower, I always take a bath," then *take* a shower. If you constantly walk or drive along the same route to get wherever you're going, try another way to get there. You'll see different terrain. You'll get glimpses of different people, different shops.

Although these may seem to be minor changes, you'll discover, surprisingly, that they give you a feeling of freshness, a new sense of aliveness. Set patterns of life, in time, dull the senses. You tend no longer to see things about you ... neither their beauty nor their ugliness.

Then, too, habituating yourself to making small changes can make you ready to face the big, often difficult changes inevitable in every life. You wouldn't think of starting with a hundred sit-ups a day if you were working toward more flexibility in your back. If you did tackle it, foolishly, you'd undoubtedly end up on some chiropractor's table, groaning in pain. But if you began with ten sit-ups a day then when the day arrived to tackle a hundred it wouldn't seem like such a herculean task. The process of gradually habituating the body is much the same if you're after flexibility of mind.

That's part one of the technique of wooing flexibility—to force yourself to break apart those concrete habits in your life.

Part two is a variation that will be equally helpful and one that you'll find equally valuable. Become capable of changing your plans swiftly and easily, without an evasive array of "I'd love to buts—"

I have a friend who I call occasionally on the spur of the moment to join me in some enterprise or other. I have yet to chalk up a success. She never can, or to put it more accurately, she never will, change her plans. I called her not too long ago to attend a brunch and a fashion show with me. She said she couldn't make it as she had a date at the beauty parlor. Now there's certainly nothing amiss with having a standing appointment each week at the beauty parlor, except that in her case, she wouldn't consider cancelling or changing it, even to do something that might be great fun. She has a set routine with her shopping and her housework, (I privately believe she has a set routine for making set routine love with her husband) and I'm sure it never occurs to her to change any one of them at any time for any reason.

At the opposite end of the spectrum is Rosa.

Rosa, like my grandmother, is one of the incredible ones. At 80, with no assistance except for her husband, who is 84, she gave a buffet supper for 16 of her club members. I just happened to call her the morning after her party.

"What are you doing?" I asked.

"I'm in the middle of doing dishes. A never-ending stack of them. Why?"

"Well, I have to drive out to the beach on business and I hoped you might come along and we'd have lunch on the water somewhere, but—"

Before I could finish the sentence, she cut in, "I'd love to! Just give me ten minutes to get gorgeous, can you?"

"Sure. But how about the dishes?"

"What dishes?"

In exactly 10 minutes she'd powdered her nose, put on her

hat, without which she never stirred from the house, and we were happily off to the beach.

On another afternoon she invited me over for coffee. With it she served me a wedge of lemon meringue pie.

"Oh, Rosa, this pie is fantastic!" I said as I lopped off a huge bite.

She smiled, obviously pleased by my enthusiasm. "Well, at least it's nice and fresh. I just baked it at midnight."

"Why on earth at midnight?"

"Why not?" she said. "There's no ordinance that limits baking to the morning or afternoon, is there?"

"Indeed there isn't!" I took another huge bite. "Marvelous." With a small grin, "Amazing how much better it is than pie baked in the morning or afternoon."

That very same week I happened to be invited to a cocktail party. Over the martinis, we got into a discussion about sleep patterns.

"I had a terrible night last night," said one man. "Tossed and whirled 'till four o'clock this morning. Then I lay there like a beached whale 'till it got light."

Whereupon another man in the group said, "I couldn't sleep either last night." He shrugged. "So what the hell, at three o'clock I got up, went outside and washed my car."

"You washed your car at three in the morning!" said the first man.

"Sure," said the second man. "Here's the moonlight coming down—and the stars winking at you—while you bend and rub and sweat ... What's the matter with you? Don't you have any romance in your miserable, crass soul!"

What a pity, I thought, that Rosa was 80 and already had a husband. She and the man who washed his car at three in the morning would make a great pair. Wondrously flexible human beings.

I'd always flattered myself on *my* flexibility. But quite by accident one night, I discovered that I wasn't as flexible as the image I'd cherished of myself. I had invited a male friend of mine to dinner and he was in the kitchen with me, nursing his scotch, watching me make the final preparations. When he made a suggestion that I change the way I was doing something or other I said, "But I *always* do it this way."

He held aloft the index finger of his left hand and proceeded to crook it several times.

Puzzled by his gesture, I said, "What does that mean? What are you trying to say?"

"I'm saying come on, be flexible. Try it the other way."

I did. And now we use this little gesture as a signal whenever signs of rigidity rear their ugly heads. I'd like to present it to you as a gift, if I may. Use it freely. It may seem like a very small gift but I wouldn't be surprised if you find it one of the most valuable ones you ever received.

6.

Travel! That magical word that conjures up visions of exotic far-away places, of colorful, happy-faced people, of exciting and unusual adventures, to all of which the pages of the travel brochure lend an added seductiveness. Those Circean brochures have a way of making the trip, to wherever it is, sound like total sheer delight and high romance. So titillating are they that those who have never traveled can't help but cry out wistfully, "Oh, if I could only travel!"

Well, be sure and make a point of luxuriating in the brochures because it is only in those pages that the trip, no matter where it's bound, is all sheer delight and high romance. Even those of you have traveled extensively and who still enjoy it will agree, I'm sure, that in actuality travel is hard, fatiguing work.

Before you ever leave your snug, comfortable home base there's that overwhelming anxiety—the anxiety that goes hand in hand with packing for a trip; what clothes to take, how much to take, how much to leave behind. Finally comes the nerve-wracking night-before-you-take-off anxiety of struggling to remember if there's any last minute chore you've overlooked—stopping the newspaper, stopping the mail, calling the home security system headquarters; if there's any indispensable item you should have packed and didn't; if you've taken enough travelers checks with you; if your passport is safely tucked into the beautifully initialed passport case you've just bought (or been given). Much of this customarily takes place, of course, in the black dead of night so that when you hop nervously out of bed to do some last minute checking, you inevitably bang your shin on the bed post or a chair that seems to have moved mysteriously out of its accustomed spot.

Then once you've bid adieu to the anxiety and you're on your way, there starts the endless waiting around in airports, (I once took a tour through India with a company called SITA which we unanimously decided could stand for nothing else but "Sitting In The Airport"), the fitful bouts of sleep in dark and dreary airplanes that are unfailingly either too hot or too cold; making razor-close connections with planes, trains busses; frantically flagging down taxis and usually being cheated by the driver; stumbling awkwardly through a new language with each new border; being forced to segue from tuppence into francs into marks into drachmas—and all within the space of perhaps three weeks.

Even if, in your travels, you don't leave the country, you're still obliged to live out of suitcases, with all too few of your precious, nearly indispensable belongings at hand and none of your precious friends. No one to call out warmly, "Hi John—nice to see you. What's up?" There are only acquaintances who barely know you and have a minimum of concern about what happens to you. Primarily because they, also, have too few of their precious belongings and friends at hand and have a maximum of concern about what happens to themselves.

But do it. I can't urge you too strongly to DO IT. Travel. By all means. Because there is much that is great fun. Much is, of course, as it's painted in the brochures, sheer delight and high romance.

But of paramount value in the experience of travel is the fact that you're shoved into being flexible. And, at the risk of being repetitious, I want to emphasize that flexibility is one of the most essential requisites in staying young. In travel, it's forced on you, whether you like it or not. You have no choice but to put up with all sorts of inconveniences; to sleep, for instance, in many different, not always so comfortable beds fighting stubborn, neck-breaking foam rubber pillows; to discover, when you arrive at a hotel, grimy and worn with fatigue, that there's been a mix-up in your reservations and your hotel room won't be available until the following night or perhaps not at all; to extend yourself, even in the throes of "traveler's trots," to make contributions of friendliness, humor, patience; to take in stride all sorts of untoward events with which travel is peppered.

On a recent trip to South America, we stored all of our luggage except for a single flight bag in our hotel in Guayaquil while we went off on a three day side trip to the Galapagos Islands. Upon returning to Guayaquil we found, to our horror, that the hotel had gone bankrupt. The police, cordoned outside to prevent looting by a sea of angry employees who had not been paid, would permit no one to enter. Our pleas, as well as the official pleas of the United States consulate, to allow us to retrieve our luggage had the same impact as a flurry of snow flakes on a granite wall. We were obliged to take off for the remainder of the tour, which was two and a half weeks, with a single flight bag as the repository of our worldly possessions. Scarcely what you'd call sheer delight and high romance.

But I discovered, to my great surprise, that it's possible to travel with only a flight bag and still relish the trip.

I'm not saying that I'd put it at the head of my preferred list of ways to travel, stripped to the bone as we were. But I was really pleased that it had happened to me. Because it was an exercise in flexibility that was impossible to come by in the usual course of events and one that was truly invaluable.

If you can afford it, travel is one of the most important techniques around to keep you young.

And incidentally, for those of you who are convinced you can't afford it, let me tell you a little story about the man who took a trip to Alaska. When he returned, a friend asked him if he'd enjoyed his trip.

"Oh, it wasn't my trip," he said. "It was actually my daughter-in-law's."

His friend was startled. "Your daughter-in-law's?"

"Sure. One day she'll inherit what little money I have and I began thinking to myself, what will she do with it when she gets her greedy little paws on it? She'll probably take a nice trip—that's what she'll do. So *I* took the trip for her."

Take your daughter-in-law's trip!

And while you're doing it, check on yourself. Are you enjoying the people? Are you enjoying the food? Are you enjoying the scenery and the difference in the look of the country through which you're traveling from the look of your own? Or are you somewhat like the Englishwoman I met traveling through Greece?

This young woman happened to be seated next to me on the bus during a city tour of Athens. When the bus came to a stop at one of the intersections she shook her head in disapproval and then said irritably to the bus driver, "I really don't see why you couldn't have printed your street signs in English so we'd know where we were."

I turned and looked at her in utter disbelief. Then, unable to restrain myself, I said, "Tell me, miss, in England do you print street signs in Greek for the benefit of the Greek tourists?"

"Why, no—of course not!" she said. For the remainder of the tour she pointedly avoided me, staring fixedly out the window.

I could never figure out why she bothered to come all the way to Greece if what she wanted to see were street signs printed in English. It would have been much more sensible and a whole lot cheaper to stay in England. From her remark it was obvious that she didn't find much delight in these foreign parts. And you know, in spite of her nice silky brunette hair and smooth, unwrinkled skin, she was old. Or rapidly en route to old age.

Fortunately she was not the rule. Many of the people I met did enjoy the country thoroughly. They were eager to see whatever there was to see—curious to explore whatever there was to explore.

And as I watched them, a thought struck me. I thought, "Those of us who are traveling through this foreign country are curious about it, fascinated by it, eager to see and do all there is to be seen and done ... because we know we probably won't be back again. Chances are we're only coming through once." And I wondered why people don't feel the same way about life. We only come through once. As far as anyone has been able to ascertain, we won't be back here again, so why shouldn't we be interested, eager, curious to see and do all there is to be seen and done?

Why not give the same avid enthusiastic interest to life as we do to a foreign country? Deserves it, don't you think? Keeps you young, too!

7.

Along with Webster's notable definition of youth—youthfully fresh in body or mind or spirit—there's another definition of youth that I happen to like very much. It's one that I came across quite a long time ago but have never forgotten because it seems to me to be such a beautifully accurate one. Like Webster's definition, it says not a word about smooth skin. Nor does it mention a strong back or 20-20 eyesight. It defines youth as a predominance of courage over timidity, of the appetite for adventure over the desire for safety.

The appetite for adventure over the desire for safety! That phrase had such a free-wheeling lilt to it that it always stayed in my memory.

To each of us, of course, adventure is bound to connote something different. To me, adventure doesn't necessitate joining a safari to Africa. Nor does it necessarily mean being the first man into space. But however you happen to conceive of adventure, you'll agree, I'm sure, that there is one central ingredient, one that all adventurous forays have in common; that is, taking a risk, taking a chance, rather than playing it safe.

It can be an adventure to do something as simple as trying a new restaurant. As small as it seems, you're taking a risk.

Believe it or not, there *are* people who wouldn't dream of stepping foot into a restaurant with which they weren't familiar. Perhaps—only perhaps—you're one of them. And if, by some chance, you should be, then it's time you abandoned the "comfort zone" and started taking a few risks.

You can begin by trying out this particular avenue of adventure: tonight—or, if you need a little time to jack up your courage, tomorrow night—walk into some restaurant with which you're totally unfamiliar, one that's completely unknown to you, even by recommendation. And while you're poring over the menu, go the whole hog. Order something that's brand-new to you, something you've never tasted before.

Leading restaurateurs agree that experimenting with a new dish is done by only the young in heart. Well-known resort owner Paul Grossinger says, "We always have the old reliable standards like steak and chops on the menu for those who don't feel young and carefree enough to try something different."

So be young and carefree! If you're strictly a steak and chops aficionado try chicken marengo. Or if bordelaise sauce is an absolute necessity to keep you happy try humble, unadorned cottage cheese.

I mentioned to a friend of mine at lunch one day that I'd eaten snails the previous night in a restaurant.

"Snails!" she gulped. Then, with a violent shudder, "Ich."

"Have you ever eaten snails?" I asked mildly.

Her retort was emphatic. "No, *ma'am.* "

"They're very good. Why don't you try them?"

She shook her head. "Couldn't. Just could *not.* " Then, with another shudder, "As each one went down, I'd be thinking of all that Snarol I'd fed them still percolating in their insides. Ich."

Well, if snails seem too drastic for you (and it's a great pity if they do) then try something else. But do try something you've never tackled before.

Or course when you order unfamiliar food, there's always the chance that you might not be happy with it. But then you just might. So you'll have not only discovered a treat for your taste buds, but in addition, you'll have made a bold stride toward being adventurous.

I find that many people succumb to the seductive allure of the routine and familiar simply because such experiences are snug and easy, and though usually dull, are safe. Whereas new experiences, even though they may be fresh and full of fun, involve thinking, effort or risk.

But I can't emphasize too strongly the necessity of *taking* risks, whether large ones or small ones, if you want to stay young.

Since I firmly believe in following my own precepts, I ordered a dish in a New York restaurant some months ago that was new to me and struck me as somewhat unusual. It was Brussels sprouts cooked with glace' chestnuts. I happen to like chestnuts very much but in combination with Brussels sprouts it gave me a little pause. However, when the dish arrived, I found that the combination was simply delicious.

When I returned to Los Angeles a few days later I gave a dinner party. As my guests were all very good cooks, some of them in the gourmet class, and I wanted to widen their eyes as well as fill their stomachs, I decided to try the Brussels sprouts and chestnuts.

I had very little notion of what went into the dish but I took my courage in hand and began. First off, I cooked the sprouts until they were almost soft. Then I dumped them into a frying pan with some butter, salt, pepper, lemon juice, a little brown sugar and the glace' chestnuts and tossed them around together for a while. (The foregoing details are for the benefit of you—my fellow chestnut lovers.)

When I served the concoction to my guests I must say I was somewhat apprehensive. But it was delicious and every one of those accomplished cooks raved. In that heady moment the words of Aeschylus flashed through my mind: "Men are not made for safe havens. The fullness of life is in the hazards of life." Although admittedly, mine was only a very minor example of adventure, still I felt a fine sense of elation.

I could imagine what King Solomon and King David felt. According to the poem by Dr. James Naylor, they tackled other, more ambitious avenues of adventure.

The poem goes:

King Solomon and King David
Led merry, merry lives
With many, many lady friends
And many, many wives.
But when the years crept over them
They had many, many qualms
So King Solomon wrote the Proverbs
And King David wrote the Psalms.

Now you might not be interested in writing the equivalent of the Proverbs or the Psalms but you can try *something* new. Go some place completely different. Buy something for yourself you've never considered buying before! Join something—perhaps a group or an organization you've never been involved with before. I urge this on you because it's so important always to be planning something. And it's important that it be new experiences you're looking forward to.

How extremely important it is you can judge from this statement that I came across in a medical journal, "A great deal of what in older people appears to be degenerative disease caused by aging is in fact functional disease, strictly the result of despair, sadness and futility." No use any longer. Nothing ahead. All over.

In 1961 there was a longevity study conducted at the Veteran's Administration outpatient clinic in Boston. The subjects of the investigation were 134 Spanish American War veterans. So remarkably healthy were the subjects, who ranged in age from 71 to 92 years, that the VA medical researchers dubbed them "the amazing octogenarians." A young X-ray technician at the clinic said, speaking of the 82 year old Frank Abbott of Massachusetts, "If I went through the paces of his daily work routine, I'd have to go to bed for a week and rest."

But to me one of the most interesting things about the study were the remarks made by James F. Cummins, the doctor who headed the project. He said that the Spanish American veterans were predominantly volunteers with ADVENTUROUS SPIRITS.

He mentioned Tom Seymour, then 82, a former master electrician. Seymour had served in Cuba and then later was part of the Signal Corps in the Klondike during the gold rush. He also mentioned Joseph McNamara, who, then 80, had only just retired from the Navy. He had seen service in two world wars and was most recently busy on recruiting duty.

"And," said Dr. Cummins, "that spirit of adventure that was typical of all of them as young men is still with them all today."

So to help insure that the spirit of adventure will always be with you, even into your 80's and 90's, there's a good technique you can make use of. Whether you're 17 or 70, it'll work wonders. Make a small cardboard sign, perhaps 9" by 11". It can be cut quite handily from the top or a dress or suit box. On it, in big bold letters, print three words—PLAN SOME-THING NEW. Then prop the placard up on your breakfast table where you'll be confronted with it each morning. Prop it up somewhere on the table so that the milk carton or the box of Wheaties won't block your view. Or hang the placard just over your bathroom mirror.

Of course, wherever you put the sign you can, if you choose, always manage, with a little effort, to ignore it. Or you can grow so accustomed to it that you no longer see it, and it just lies around, unheeded, gathering dust. Wily dodges, these—but dodges you can ill afford if you've chosen to cast your lot on the side of staying young.

The other half of what constitutes youth, according to the definition, is the predominance of courage over timidity.

Courage, as we're all aware, is that quality of mind which enables one to encounter danger and difficulties without paralyzing fear or fainting of heart. This is a good one to practice because we all tend to dread facing any difficulties in our lives; as the years go along we all tend more and more to face even the changes with dread. Well, as it so happens, there are inevitably all sorts of difficulties and changes in every life. We have no choice about that. But we do have a choice about the way we meet the changes.

I have a friend named Lillian. Lillian did an enormous amount of complaining about her apartment. She had lived in it for over 15 years and always "the closet space was completely inadequate," "the kitchen was dark as a dungeon," she "didn't have a broom closet" and "the approach was so ugly." But each time I'd mildly suggest that she look for another apartment, she'd change the subject.

One day she called me in a veritable panic. It seemed she'd received a notification that they were tearing down the apartment house where she lived to make room for a parking lot and all the tenants were being evicted.

"But Lil," I said, "you always disliked that apartment so. Why are you upset about leaving?"

"Well, it's such a shock—"

"Yes, of course. That I can well understand."

She went on, "And I'm so used to this place—and I have no idea where I can go ..."

"Oh, come on, Lillian, you'll find another apartment without too much..."

She cut in sharply, "It's all very well for you to talk. You're not in this terrible spot." And she banged up the receiver.

The anguish that she proceeded to put herself through for the next few weeks was fearful to behold. But as it turned out, being evicted was the face of Providence beaming down at her with one of its most dazzling smiles. Not only did she find a very nice apartment with lavish closet space, a sunny kitchen and a complete service porch, but it was in a small triplex which she was able to buy. And as icing on the cake, the triplex has by now quadrupled in value.

When Lillian told me happily about her new apartment I couldn't help but think of my struggle with the fly. Occasionally I find a fly in my house and invariably it seems to settle on the sliding glass doors leading to the patio. Rather than swat it and splatter the fly all over the glass I slide open one of the doors and attempt to shoo the fly out. There, just outside, is sun and space and freedom! But it buzzes obstinately to the corner of the door furthest from the open space I've provided for his exit. Some few do take advantage of the safe conduct pass. But most of the flies battle frantically and fearfully against the very thing that is to their best interest. And, of course, end up getting clobbered.

But then situations can't always turn out as felicitously as did my friend Lillian's. If, though, whatever your situation and however fearsome it seems, you can dredge up sufficient courage at the very outset to look on it not as a disaster but as a challenge, at least some part of your misery will be mitigated.

That's not an easy stance to take, I'll admit. But whoever said life was easy? Any time you find yourself wishing that it were, just bear in mind, or better still, write it down and keep it on your bedside table, the quotation from Seneca. The old Roman said, in 65 A.D., "Life without perturbation and without misadventure is like a dead sea."

So when perturbation and misadventure come your way, and you can be absolutely certain that they will, don't shrink from them—or wail over them—or let your heart go into an erratic trot. SALUTE THEM. Don't hop back behind those frightened, doleful phrases, "How will I possibly work this out?" or "I just cannot face this problem!" or "*What* am I going to do now?" That line of thinking is not only an utter waste of time but, more importantly, your panic will paralyze you and thus succeed in choking off any possibility of your coping.

"Working out this situation will be a real *challenge!*" Let that be your attitude. "Facing this problem is a *challenge!*" Choose that as your attitude.

At the same time keep in the forefront of your mind the fact that life crises are nature urging you to a new level of strength, forcing you toward the full development of your inner resources, even though in certain instances it's virtually impossible to see how. As in the life crisis that involves the death of a loved one. That is probably the most difficult of all changes to accept. And yet even there you have a choice of attitude. You can, after the initial period of mourning, choose to withdraw from life, as had several widows I met in a seminar I attended. These women had all been widowed for two to three years and yet not one of them would venture out at night, since in the past they'd always been accompanied by their husbands. They weren't involved in cultivating any new activities or even interested in many of the old ones; they were too busy bemoaning the fact that their particular group of friends, all of them couples, no longer included them in their outings, as they had in the past.

But there is an alternative choice in facing the loss of a loved one and that's the choice my neighbor made. Although her marriage had been one of the best I've ever known, after a few months of desperate grief, she faced up to the fact that the marriage was irrevocably ended and began to pick up her life. Accepting, rather than resenting, the inescapable fact that she no longer had any place in the world of couples, she turned for friendship to her single acquaintances, some of them widowed, some divorced. With their support, she signed up for an exercise class, she started studying for a real estate license (even though money was no problem in her case) and bit by bit she rebuilt her life around other fulcrums than the physical presence of her husband.

It was heart-warming to watch her courageously transforming this traumatic change into a challenge. Incidentally, it's interesting to note how close those two words are. The word "change" becomes the word "challenge" merely by splitting it down the middle and inserting three letters 'lle'. Presto—change is now challenge!

Of course it's not quite that easy to convert an actual life change into a challenge. But I promise you that if you *can* do it you'll feel at once a tiny bit more powerful, a tiny bit more capable of dealing with whatever it is that needs must be dealt with. For managing to make a change inevitably generates a feeling of increased self-esteem. So even if at first your heart's not in it, if at first you feel you must shrink and wail, then shrink and wail. But for no longer than you find absolutely necessary. Then catch hold of the "challenge" technique once more and hang on tight.

Each time you make this about-face from timidity to courage you'll discover making it a little less difficult. Until gradually the metamorphosis becomes habitual and when a problem of whatever stripe confronts you, your attitude will, surprisingly enough, be automatically one of saluting, rather than pulling back. You might even get to the place where you'll be able to view some of the "perturbations and misadventures" that befall you as interesting, rather than letting them crush you to the ground with their enormity.

At this juncture your courage will have so outstripped your timidity that it's almost inevitable for people to exclaim in admiration, "Oh, him, or her, or them—as the case may be—they're so gutsy they'll never be old." And you know—you won't.

8.

The late president of Columbia College, Nicholas Murray Butler, made what I consider quite an amazing and somewhat frightening statement. He said that in his experience and observation, both of which of course were extensive, only a small minority of human beings continued to grow intellectually after they reached the age of—not 50 or 60 or 70—but after the age of 23 or 24. He said he found they settled down then to fixed habits of mind, fixed points of view, permanent likes and dislikes; that they built walls about themselves behind which they continue to exist as long as life lasted.

Mr. Butler's observation is supported by that of the famous European physiologist Rubner who said some 50 years ago that man's most significant aging starts when he goes to work. This early aging, Rubner explains, is the result of "sinking into purely occupational tasks, neglecting any further development of the self, narrowing of the mental horizons."

"But my work is very demanding and time-consuming," an executive will tell you.

His wife may say, "But the children and the house and the chores that must be done take practically all my energy."

Or, from a wage earner comes, "But I'm worn out when I get home at the end of the day."

In all of these statements there is certainly some validity. However, I have a small suspicion that there's still another element that's hiding behind this "narrowing of the mental horizons"; another element responsible for this "neglect of the development of the self." That other element is inertia.

That's the old devil that's in there every second cajoling softly, "Come on, sit back—take it easy—you're tired. Natural-

ly. You work hard—you're not made of cast iron, you know..."
And then as the years roll by, the words start to vary
somewhat. "Come on, you've done your share—you're entitled
now to do less—you have a perfect right to sit back." Most
solicitous, most convincing talk.

However, the obligato running beneath those solicitous,
seductive words is another matter entirely. In actuality what
the devil is trilling in your ear, no matter what your age, is that
you're entitled to stagnate, that you have a right to start rotting. And that wily, persuasive devil is exactly on target. You
do have a right to start rotting. You *are* entitled to stagnate.
IF you choose. And the choice is entirely yours. You can start
rotting and stagnating. Or, on the other hand, once more the
choice is yours, you can boot the luckless devil right down the
nearest flight of stairs.

Cicero, in his marvelous essay on OLD AGE, gives some
practical clues on how to go about accomplishing this feat. Into the mouth of his character, Cato, who is 80 years of age, he
puts the following words, "I am busy composing the seventh
book of my origins and getting my speeches into shape for
publication. I am writing treatises on civil law and I have
started studying Greek. Each evening I repeat whatever I
have said, or heard, or done in the course of the day, just to
keep my memory in working order. The man who is always living in the midst of such efforts keeps his mind at full stretch,
like a bow, and never gives in to age by becoming slack."

Exactly as did Nicholas Murray Butler many years later,
Cicero observed that as we go along we have a tendency to let
our mental horizons become more and more narrowed. And it's
for this reason that he has his character Cato list his
multifarious pursuits, ranging all the way from composing a
book to studying Greek. In other words, he is infused with the
determination to stretch his mind.

Now I'm not advocating that you study Greek necessarily.
But I am advocating, and with the utmost urgency, that you
search out and become involved in some course of study.
Preferably choose a course that has no connection with your
occupation, and preferably a course that is brand new to you,
as a means of stretching your mind.

If, as you read this, you don't find yourself burning with enthusiasm to begin studying some course, then pick up the telephone and call one of your local high schools. Ask them to send you their adult education brochure for the following semester. Or if there is a university close by, telephone or write them and request that you be put on the mailing list for their catalog. Somewhere in that vast array of pages there's bound to be a course, perhaps even two, that will kindle some sort of fire under you.

As important and as profitable as you might concede this line of action to be, you still may not find it all that easy to pursue. For inertia is always in there, doing its insidious work. That urge to sit back, to stop striving and coast along is inordinately powerful. And, what's more, it usually gathers strength with the years.

I'm sure that most of you have felt a touch of it at one time or another. I know I have. But what makes the critical difference between one life and another is that some people give into that fatal inertia and some defy it. They battle inertia with all the weapons in their arsenal. And those of you who are determined to keep your youth *must* battle it. You cannot afford to quit striving—ever.

I'm reminded of the words of the small boy who said, "My father can climb the highest mountain. He can swim the broadest river. He can do almost anything! But most of the time he just throws out the garbage." Oh, it's wonderfully comfortable to sit back and just throw out the garbage most of the time. But the comfort gradually becomes apathy, boredom and, eventually, inevitably, old age.

In the newspapers a few years ago there was a story about a couple by the name of Allen and Pearl Purchis who were awarded their high school diplomas at the respective ages of 81 and 82. Attending their graduation ceremony in Lansing, Michigan, were five of their seven children, eight of their 24 grandchildren and two of their great-grandchildren.

The couple admitted that several times during their schooling they were sorely tempted to drop out. But they had committed themselves to earning a diploma and even though it wasn't easy to keep at it, it wasn't easy for them to drop out either. "For whenever we thought of quitting," Mrs. Purchis recalled with a smile, "we realized our whole caboodle of kids would, of course, know it and it sure wouldn't set a very good example. Especially for the grandchildren."

Her husband added, "They'd have read us the riot act all right if we had!"

So the pair stuck it out and graduated in the top thirty percent of their class.

I fervently hope that the gentleman whose conversation I overheard recently in a hotel lobby happens to read this book. Or at least dips into it long enough to come across the story of Allen and Pearl Purchis.

This man was saying to his friend with some wistfulness, "Sure wish I'd gone to college."

His friend asked, "Why don't you go now?"

The man shrugged. "Aw, I've got a wife and kids and a job. It'd take me 10 years to get through college now."

His friend asked, "How old will you be in 10 years?"

"I'll be 50!"

With a sly look, his friend asked, "And how old will you be in 10 years if you don't go to college?"

"Fifty..." The man smiled a little sheepishly, "Hey, what do you know, it's exactly the same!"

Unlike this gentleman, the Purchises were not in the least deterred from starting their education by the thought that it would take them too long to finish. And they certainly weren't put off by the commonly held, ramshackle notion that they were too old to tackle such a project. They chose a track to traverse and, despite some attacks of second-thought along the way, triumphantly went the distance.

This doesn't mean that attendance at school for the remainder of your life is a ramrod requisite. It's entirely possible, if you so prefer, to study on your own. Some people have managed it quite successfully. However, there are many advantages to learning in a class with other people. For one, you're bound to be stimulated by the competition. For another, you'll enjoy the contacts with men and women you wouldn't encounter in the ordinary course of your life. You're also committed to a particular course of study, whatever it may happen to be, and you won't be as quick to abandon it as you might if you were studying alone. That's quite an attractive assemblage of fringe benefits, to my way of thinking.

But however you decide to study, whether in a class or alone, whether it's difficult for you or not, very shortly, I believe, you'll find youself somehow aglow with a feeling of great personal accomplishment. I discovered quite some time ago, that with learning there comes this sense of personal accomplishment. Some of you may have already experienced that lovely feeling. You may have been suffused with its warmth. You may be aware of how exhilarating it is; how much more alive it makes you; how much better an outlook on life it gives you.

And there is yet one more value in learning, quite an impressive one. It's not only that you profit by scraping an aquaintanceship with new facts, which is exciting in itself, but researchers working in this area have uncovered a bonanza that becomes yours as well. Their findings are that learning generates a hefty increase in your total overall alertness and a very noticeable speedup in the entire gamut of your responses.

Then, of course, the bottom line is my favorite quotation. It's from Aeschylus, who said many centuries ago, "To learn what is new is to be forever young."

9.

"Interests," says H.A. Overstreet in his book THE MATURE MAN, "are the links that join us to the mainstream of life." Not only do they serve to join us to the mainstream of life but they also accomplish another very important purpose. They enable us to skirt the quagmire of old age. Without an interest, a keen and thoughtful interest, in at least some of the more visible things in the world about you: in current events, in the many new and exciting developments in the fields of science, medicine, and art, you are already sloshing around in the backwater of life.

You're no longer just sloshing around but you're up to your knees in that brackish backwater if you find yourself looking to your husband, your wife, your children or to anyone else to provide you with some sort of life, a kind of vicarious existence, simply because your own interests are so shockingly minimal or even, more tragically, totally nonexistent.

There's a little story that I feel is apropos here about a middle aged couple who lived in a small apartment hotel. One morning the wife said to her husband indignantly, "I'm sure tempted to move out of this hotel. The whole place is rotten!"

Mildly her husband replied, "Why, I don't think so. What makes you say that?"

"Well, in the very next room to ours from what I heard last night ..." she broke off, her brows raised in fierce disapproval.

Her husband said placatingly, "Oh, you can't judge from an occasional word that you hear."

Whereupon the wife snorted, "Occasional word nothing! Why, these walls are thin as paper. All you have to do is put your ear right up close against 'em and you can't miss a single

43

syllable!''

Living life? Well, I suppose you *could* call it that. But it's a pretty thin, completely vicarious sort of life.

However, you'll never be caught in the deadly trap of any second-hand existence if you're occupied in constantly, steadily forging links to the mainstream of life. You'll have neither the time nor the need to flatten your ears against any one else's walls.

There's a little technique I recommend to give you exact bearings on how far you've waded out into the backwater of life. You might find it worth your while to try it.

Add up your interests. I'm not advocating that you run them over in your mind and let it go at that. Sit down with a pencil and a sheet of paper. Down the middle of the paper draw a line. On one side put the heading, THINGS THAT IN-TEREST ME—AND THAT I *DO*. On the other side of the paper, THINGS THAT MIGHT POSSIBLY INTEREST ME —AND THAT I *DON'T* DO. Then spend time filling it out in complete detail. It could be something of a revelation to you.

I suggested to a man once that he do this exercise. And on the side of the ledger headed, THINGS THAT INTEREST ME—AND THAT I DO, was a single line. "I look forward to supper," he'd written, "looking at television for a while and going to bed." He was 53 years old and that's all that living held for him.

When he reread the sheet of paper after he'd finished with it I noticed a puzzled frown crease his brow. I doubt that until that very moment he'd given any thought to the meagreness of his life. And it must have seemed particularly meagre to him when he actually saw on paper the paucity of the things he enjoyed side by side with the long list of interests that were possible to him but that had no place in his life. Whether he ever decided to do anything about remedying that pathetically meagre life I have no way of knowing.

And if, by any chance, when you finish your list, it happens to have the same lopsided look as his, remember it's you, and only you, that can change its shape. And remember, too, that when you do, you'll change your life.

At the age of 80, Oliver Wendell Holmes made the statement, "I find new vistas opening all around me." You can be sure that the illustrious Justice Holmes started early in life to develop interests or at 80 he couldn't possibly have still found new vistas opening all around him.

I'm not aware of what all of his interests were but there's a story told about him which certainly pinpoints one of them. When he was 90 he was out strolling with a male friend and a very beautiful girl passed them. Mr. Holmes turned to look at her, then turning back to his companion said wistfully, "Ah, to be 70 again!" Quite obviously the side of his ledger headed THE THINGS THAT INTEREST ME included the ladies.

So may yours. And that is indeed a stroke of fortune. Because it's practically impossible to get old while you have a good, thirsty interest in sexuality.

Of course, having a good, thirsty interest isn't limited solely to sex. With a good, thirsty interest in almost anything there's not much chance of your getting old.

Some people just "luck out." Their interests are strongly marked, easy for them to determine. For example, a young gynecologist I know, who had always enjoyed working with wood, apprenticed himself to a skilled cabinet maker. Now his deft hands are turning out beautiful furniture—as well as beautiful hysterectomies. An accountant of my acquaintance has become, with study and countless field trips to the desert, an expert rock hound. And still another doctor, now retired, is displaying the same cleverness in diagnosing disease in plants as he did in diagnosing illness in his human patients.

My neighbor was sitting in her patio one morning scrawling laboriously in a notebook. As I sauntered past I said, "That looks mighty like shorthand."

She glanced up from the notebook and smiled. "Right on the nose. I'm trying to learn shorthand."

"Anything special in mind?"

She shrugged. "I don't know, I might become a court reporter. Always seemed like an interesting sort of life to me."

The footnote to this particular story is that the lady studying shorthand happened to be 85 years old.

Of course you just may not be entranced by the idea of becoming a rock hound or a court reporter. It's possible you're not one of those who "lucked out." You might not have a natural bent or inclination in any direction. However, I've found that if you keep looking persistently for something that appeals to you, something somehow will come your way.

You *could* stumble onto something wonderfully absorbing, as did a good friend of mine, just by utilizing the trial and error method.

She said to me one day, "You know, I'd sure like to have some sort of hobby—but I haven't the vaguest notion of what."

"Want to talk about it?"

"Yeah, let's do. Because I'm really intrigued by those theories of yours."

We tossed ideas back and forth for a while and finally she decided she'd take up dressmaking. For a time she tried her hand at it. But she didn't particularly cotton to it. Then she signed up for a course in ceramics. After she'd filled her house and my house and the houses of most of her friends and relatives with strangely shaped ashtrays and salt and pepper shakers that leaked all over the table cloth, she concluded that ceramics was not for her either.

Finally, quite by chance, she stumbled on a hobby that really caught her fancy.

We were walking together one day when we passed a bush laden with small orange flowers. For a few moments we stood looking at it, speculating about what sort of bush it was. My friend insisted it was lantana.

"No, it's not lantana," I said.

"Oh yes it is."

From the Olympian heights of authority I handed down, "I have lantana growing in my garden and the flowers are lavender."

"Want to bet?"

"Sure. Ten dollars."

"One dollar," she said. "I don't want to steal your money."

Well, I happened to be woefully ignorant of the fact that only some lantana bushes bear lavender flowers. The blooms of others are orange. I lost my dollar.

Somehow this incident awakened her interest in bushes and trees. She bought a small paperback book and took it on her walks. With the help of the text and the pictures scattered through the book she managed to identify many of the trees and bushes she passed. She acquired a great many more books, pored over them and expanded her knowledge. Today she's an enthusiastic authority on botany.

So much for the mechanics of the trial and error technique. If you're among those who, like my friend, are intrigued by my theories but are bewildered about where to begin, you might give this technique a try.

A field that's a fertile one from which to cull an idea is the hobby show. Track down one of those in your area.

You're in luck if you happen to live anywhere in the vicinity of Cleveland, Ohio. There's a first rate hobby show that's been presented in Cleveland annually for the past 14 years. Also, in Concord, New Hampshire, the League of New Hampshire Arts and Crafts sponsors an annual Craftsmens' Fair. Something there might strike a spark in you.

A couple of years ago, in Lacey, Washington, I was a speaker at the convention of the Air Stream Trailer club. The club, composed of people from all over the country who own Air Stream trailers, holds its convention each year in a different locale. It's well worth it to locate one of these. They have sociable dinners, entertainment and a hobby display by which I'm sure you'll be struck and completely enchanted, as I was. Not only is it a very large display, but the hobbies represented were so unusual and the articles exhibited, many of them for sale, were so beautiful that I made a special point of being introduced to several of the members responsible for them. When I met them, I was not in the least surprised to discover that practically without exception they were interested, happy, alive individuals, enthusiastic about their hobbies and taking enormous pride in the end product which had obviously demanded so great an expenditure of time and meticulous work.

Of course you may be one of those convivial people who prefer a hobby that doesn't necessitate time spent alone, a hobby that allows you to consort with others. Some good friends of mine, a charming young couple, fell into that category. They were totally enamored of traveling but since their income was limited they were able to manage very few trips. So they hit on the notion of organizing, as their hobby, an armchair travel club.

In no time at all they'd gathered around them quite a good-sized and most enterprising group of friends who were all delighted with the notion. This is how it worked: the participants in the group would take turns pairing off and selecting a trip to some foreign country with which they were wholly unfamiliar. The pair would then collect travel brochures, pictures, postage stamps and guide books dealing with the country; they would dig out library books written about the area and acquaint themselves with its history, background and customs; they would attend travelogues to flesh out their knowledge. Eventually they would make up their itinerary, choose the best modes of transportation, find out where visas were required (travel agents, they discovered, were very nice about helping), decide on a wardrobe suitable for the upcoming climate as well as the length of the trip, in short, do everything that was necessary for the projected journey—except go.

Then, when the "travelers" returned they would host a festive dinner party featuring the national food and drink of the country they'd just visited and after dinner one or both of them would regale the group with a comprehensive and entertaining rundown of their "trip."

A most original sort of hobby, I thought—and one that was also a veritable storehouse of ancillary benefits: it was fun; it was instructive; it stimulated the imagination, for seeing to it that the account of the trip was amusing as well as factual meant conjuring up all sorts of imaginary anecdotes; it supplied practice in flouting the fear that statistics show, surprisingly, is number one on the list of all fears—speaking before a group. And finally, it fulfilled the requisites for any hobby that is not just a narcotic to kill time—diligent application and fresh learning. My friends, who hadn't been aware of all the ramifications when they'd initiated the project, were completely enthralled with their brain child.

But even if you're not blanketed with enthusiasm, even if you take part in some project reluctantly or half-heartedly, it's surprising how swift Nature is to give you a hand. She seems to work right along with you so that quite quickly you find yourself developing an interest in it, and real satisfaction.

For instance, I know a man who buys old houses and fixes

them up for resale. He's most creative. He knocks out walls here and there, puts in sliding glass doors, repapers, repaints, does all sorts of lovely things that require vision, imagination and, of course, money. I was with him one day when he stopped to show me an old house that he was considering buying. Subsequently he bought it and several times, as work progressed on the house, I went by to look at it. I became very interested in seeing the house change, take on a prettier and more modish appearance. It was not only fascinating to watch but I managed to pick up quite a bit of knowledge about remodeling.

When the time arrived to put the house on the market I was as eager about seeing it sell as was my friend who owned the house. And I was almost as excited as he was about the price it brought. You see, I'd invested in the project. I'd invested my time, thought and interest and so I'd reaped a return in enjoyment and added knowledge.

You can't escape reaping some reward when you invest—in anything. Even though your expertise is limited and the time you spend at it not appreciable, *any* interest you tuck under your belt becomes a good investment. If you've ever played tennis, though you may have only clumped around the court and spent as much time chasing after the ball as hitting it, you enjoy watching a tennis tournament infinitely more than someone who has never held a racket. And if you can play the piano, even though the extent of your ability may be only a sketchy rendition of HOME ON THE RANGE, hearing a piano concert will be a greater pleasure to you than to a person who has no first-hand knowledge of the instrument. After I'd picked up playing the guitar, I bought some of the records of that great master, Segovia. And I'd listen to them intently. It opened up a whole new vista for me. I'd never paid much attentin to the guitar before. Now it was a brand-new avenue of pleasure.

One of my friends is dabbling in painting. I asked her the other day when she expected to have her first one-woman show.

"Van Gogh I am completely and unequivocally not," she said. "Just between you and me, I have one thimbleful of talent. But I do enjoy it. And you know, the most amazing thing, fooling around with painting has opened up to me a whole new world of color. When I go to a gallery nowadays I see things that I never noticed before. For instance, I see the myriad array of colors in a portrait of a face that I'd always taken for granted was just one single shade. It's really quite exciting."

And it is, you'll find.

Even marriage is bound to be a happier and more vital experience for those of you who are fortunate enough to be part of that charmed circle who, no matter what their age, find "new vistas opening all around them." For your marriage can grow, as marriage must if it is to be more than just endured, because is has something to grow with and to grow upon. It's not likely to become contracted and stale and monotonous.

I knew of one couple who felt, and rightly so, that a youthful attitude was merely another name for pioneering in a different area. So when either of them felt disinterested in life or felt that their relationship was becoming dulled he or she would suggest to the partner that they enlarge their field of interests. Neither of them subscribed to the notion, firmly held by many married couples, that recapturing their zest in living necessitated capturing a new sexual partner. They were both wise enough to recognize, as they phrased it, "the trouble and dangers inherent in that sort of short-term exercise in futility." Instead, they would manage to find a stimulating lecture to attend together, learn German or French or Chinese cooking together. The last time I talked to them they were on their way to a weekend seminar given by the Society for the Scientific Study of Sex, where papers were to be read by doctors, psychologists and counselors on every aspect of sex.

Always they were involved in some sort of renewal of zestful experiences. Hence, their love and their marriage remained interesting because they saw to it that the world, that is, the world that *they* inhabited, was always interesting.

To sustain a fresh and interesting marriage the two people involved must lead interesting lives. This doesn't mean necessarily glamorous lives or unusual lives or lives photographed constantly by Ron Galella. What it does mean is that the marriage partners must be constantly interested. If they're not, then monogamous and monotonous become synonymous and eventually add up to—old.

Not only is it first-rate insurance for your marriage to initiate and sustain interests. It also happens to be first-rate insurance for your health.

There was a survey conducted in New York not long ago which found that when a group of older people became active in a full-time day center their visits to a medical clinic fell off seventy-nine percent. When I read that, it seemed an unbelievable statistic. But it was a most heartening and exciting one.

Dr. Gershon Lesser hosted a weekly radio program in Los Angeles and he told an extraordinary story on his show about a doctor who had just taken over the post of medical director for a convalescent hospital. When the new director made a tour of the hospital and saw the condition of the patients he was horrified. Most of them, dressed in hospital garb, lay stretched out dully on their beds, dull eyes staring at the ceiling, dull ears unresponsive to the entrance of doctors, of nurses, often even to the members of the family.

One of the first official moves the new doctor made was to issue a directive that each patient was to have four ounces of beer every day at three o'clock.

In a very short time some patients who had been just picking at their food started to eat. Others who had been lying on their beds in an almost catatonic state began to sit up and wait for the beer.

Then the doctor changed his orders. The beer was to be served only in the general recreation room.

There was a wave of protest about this, especially from those patients who hadn't been out of bed in months. But they got up finally and hobbled out of their rooms. They had no choice if they wanted the beer. And they wanted the beer. Hair that had been straggling and wispily unkempt for some time began to be combed and brushed into a semblance of order. And every day at two-thirty, half an hour before the beer was due to be served, the recreation room was already three-quarters full.

Gradually the patients started talking to one another, some even laughing a little together. And just one year from the time the doctor first issued his order, the hospital chapel, which had never been used for any purpose before was the setting for a wedding. The bride was 72, the groom 81. At the reception following the wedding there was no champagne served. Beer, felt the happy bride and groom, was in this instance much more fitting.

And thus endeth Dr. Lesser's lovely fairy tale, which differs from all other fairy tales in that it just happens to be true.

Dr. Smiley Blanton, a psychiatrist, who wrote the book *Now or Never*, underlines how extremely crucial interests are to your health. He says flatly, "I have never seen a single case of senility in people, no matter how old, as long as they maintained an active interest in other human beings and in things outside of themselves."

A formidable statement, to my way of thinking. And I don't know about you, but it's one that makes a real impact on me. Because I have encountered senility in people close and dear to me. Perhaps some of you have too. And if so, I'm sure you'll agree that it's a state to be avoided at any cost.

For years it was believed that the primary cause of senility was cerebral arteriosclerosis. But, according to both Dr. Blanton and a series of post-mortem studies, that is completely untrue. These studies have proven that some people who were alert and vigorous at the time of their death had a high degree of hardening of the arteries to the brain while others who were senile had comparatively youthful brains.

This surprising finding plus the skilled observations of people like Dr. Martin Symonds, a psychiatrist at Bellevue Hospital from 1955 to 1957 and subsequently on the staff of the Karen Horney Clinic, led research staffs to come to practically the same conclusion as did Dr. Blanton: that those people who retain a place in life, who have a modicum of importance, who keep up keen interests and a certain amount of responsibilities, are not likely to become senile no matter what the condition of their brain arteries.

Perhaps some of you may choose to disparage the findings of these eminent men and still feel that *you* can somehow manage to completely sidestep the major curse of becoming old and senile. Unlikely. However, if you should happen to pull it off, it's even more unlikely that you'll manage to sidestep the minor curse of becoming a tiresome old bore, the species of which are many and highly diversified.

An acquaintance of mine happens to be a member in good standing of one of the commoner varieties.

I was in the hospital recuperating from an operation when this woman dropped in to visit. She was just barely able to come out with "Hello darling, how are you feeling?" and deposit a bunch of flowers on my bedside table before launching into an account, minutely documented, of her own operation in this very hospital seven years before.

I was stunned. If there's one time when you're entitled to be the star of the drama it's when you've just been carved open and are flat on your back. But my role of stardom was totally usurped; I found myself suddenly shoved into the audience instead of lying center stage.

The writer, I.A.R. Wylie, calls these people the hypochondriac bores. Almost inevitably they have little interest in things outside themselves. Instead they are wholly preoccupied, even enraptured, with their insides. Like my visitor, whose eyes were glowing and whose whole being was throbbing with excitement as she regaled me with the data on her seven-year-old surgery.

Of course it's not always that these hypochondriac bores are in the happy position of having an operation to their credit. If not, then they'll resort to giving you an explicit, thoroughly detailed rundown on the state of their bowels, or their sinuses, or they'll inform you in sepulchral tones how concerned their doctor is about their blood pressure. It seems to be a fairly reliable fact that the less a person's interests absorb them, the more do their organs.

Almost as ubiquitous as the hypochondriac bore is the variety I've dubbed the Tuesday-Wednesday bore. These are the people who are unable to give an account of any event without laboring over the exact day it took place.

"It was last Wednesday when—" then they'll break off and make a fresh start, "No, it was Tuesday, I think..." but after a moment's careful rumination, "No, it had to be Wednesday. I remember now because I know just exactly where I was and what I was doing on Wednesday. I ..." at which point it will surely take all of your will power to prevent yourself from crying out irascibly, "What *difference* does it possibly make whether it was Tuesday or Wednesday? Tell the story!"

If, by some chance, you're so fortunate as not to have encountered one of the Tuesday-Wednesday bores, it's outside the realm of possibility that you've entirely escaped one of the "grandchildren" bores. For some reason, this category seems to be made up predominantly of women.

A neighbor of mine told me that on a recent cruise she was lying in her deck chair one morning when a woman sat down in the chair just next to hers.

Brightly the woman said, "Good morning."

My neighbor, who veers to the crotchety side, retorted, "Good morning. And please don't show me any pictures of your grandchildren."

I was completely taken aback by the brusqueness of her unprovoked offensive. However, better that, I thought, than cooing politely over pictures of perfectly strange babes in whom you have no interest whatsoever, as I myself have done on occasion when I've been cornered by these "grandchildren" bores.

I'm sure Winston Churchilll would have been thoroughly delighted by my neighbor's story since apparently he too had been victimized by the "grandchildren" bores. It is said that an ambassador once remarked to him, "You know, Sir Winston, I have never told you about my grandchildren." Whereupon Mr. Churchill beamed at him and shot back quickly, "I realize it, my dear fellow, and I just can't tell you how grateful I am!"

It so happened that Mr. Churchill was given a heaven-sent opportunity and was quick-witted enough to capitalize on it. But ordinarily, there's only one thing you can do about the bores in any of these categories and that is bear with them. Oh yes—there *is* one other thing you can do. You can employ stern precautionary measures to make certain you never join their ranks.

Leave those pictures at home. Of if you don't want to do that, then don't pull them out and foist them on unwary people.

When you tell an anecdote, don't bother struggling to recall the exact moment it took place. "Last week" or "A few days ago" will usually do beautifully.

However, better yet, and simpler really, is to see to it that your life is so full and rich with satisfying interests that you won't have to give a thought to avoid being caught in any one of the profusion of bore categories. You will just automatically avoid them.

In the life of everyone, no matter what his age, who has vowed never to allow himself to become old, there are two rules pertaining to the forging of interests that I consider most important.

Rule One: Don't postpone for one second gathering interests. Don't under any circumstances, hide behind that flyblown phrase, "Oh, I intend to do all that later." Because when is later? Generally, too late. Delete phrases like that from your vocabulary. Throw out those other phrases, too, such as, "I'll look into that when I have more time..." and, "When I get around to it." Substitute instead, "I'll start doing that right now." And even if you have three kids under the age of 10 or you're president of an international company, you can at least make a start. It's very much easier, at a later date, to pick up and polish an interest into which you've already made inroads than it is to try to start on one cold.

Rule Two: Never say "I can't" to any idea that pops into your head to try or to any suggestion that's tossed into your lap. No matter how wild it may seem, if the idea appeals to you, say, "Sure, I can do that." Then say, "And I *will* do it." And then go ahead and do it.

10.

There's a story told about a young man who had a profoundly pessimistic outlook on life. Nothing, according to his lights, was of much value, except for astrology. His faith in astrology was staunch and unwavering. Religiously each day he followed the precepts of his horoscope. One day when his horoscope read "Make new friends and see what happens," he went straight out and made three new friends. But nothing happened. Now he complains bitterly that he's stuck with three new friends!

Whether you're a devotee of astrology or not—whether, like this young fellow you're a profound pessimist or not—go right out and get yourself stuck with three new friends, or four or even five. Making new friends is a shimmering thread in the fabric of youth.

If you'll notice, children do it automatically. They make new friends easily in classes, riding the seesaw, clambering over the jungle gym, playing baseball or hide-and-seek. They never rear back from it, complain that it's difficult. It's only the people who are old—or already sliding rapidly into old age—who are reluctant about it.

Do you happen to be one of the reluctant or even remiss ones? Do you find that you keep the current circle of your friends sacrosanct. Do you ever catch yourself resorting to that handy phrase, "Well, it's so much harder to make friends as you get older," which translates, of course, into, "It's just too much trouble to make friends as you get older." Whenever it's said to me I object vehemently, at which point the speaker almost invariably dons a smug look and says, "Just wait, you'll find out one day."

Well, they've got the wrong lady. Because I never intend to find out. I don't go along with the theory that it's harder to make friends as you get older. It's only harder, or too much trouble, if you're "old." If you've allowed yourself to get old, you've allowed yourself to become unproductive, stagnant, impoverished. And in that case, it is harder, and too much trouble, because you have so little of value to contribute to a friendship.

Rather than joys, interests and enthusiasm eagerly shared, people who have permitted themselves to get old use others only as avenues of relief from their boredom; as troughs in which to pour out their troubles and complaints; as crutches on which to lean for help.

On the chance that you're interested in protecting yourself against ever becoming a part of this chilling realm, I think you'll welcome the technique I recommend. It's a simple, but a valuable one: see to it without fail that you make one friend each year of your life.

To make a new friend is an unparalleled way to stretch your horizons. It's an effective exercise in heading off stagnation, getting other points of view, opening up uncharted avenues. It's a clear, flowering path to fresh experiences.

Some of you, reading this, may say, "Why, I make loads of new friends every year!" My congratulations. You are in truth fortunate. But of you who are not in this category I would like to ask: have you made one new friend each year thus far?

It could be that some of you think it's too late since you're up there on the age scale, chronologically. But keep in mind the remark made by the 85 year-old gentleman who was learning to play the flute. When a friend said to him, "Isn't it a little late to start learning the flute at the age of 85?" he retorted, "At what lesser age can I begin, pray tell?"

And so with making new friends.

The writer, Samuel Johnson, said, "If a man does not make new acquaintances as he advances through life, he will soon find himself alone. A man, sir, should keep his friendships in constant repair." It's not only that you might, as Mr. Johnson warns, find yourself alone if you don't. You might find yourself old.

Naturally, your friends of long standing are dear. They've

been tried and tested in all sorts of difficult circumstances. I have one friend who said to me not long ago, "You know, I really don't like going to parties at anyone's house any more who's not an old friend. If I have a few drinks too many and fall asleep in the chair after dinner, as of late I've been in the habit of doing, the old friends will say and fondly too, 'Oh well, good old Helene, she's had a little too much tonight.' But the new friend will more than likely say, 'What did you think of that old lush at the party last night! What was her name again?'"

However, you have to keep in mind that the new friend will be an old friend one day. In time he might even become that rarity, a real friend who, if I may quote Samuel Johnson once again, is "one who will tell you of your faults and follies in prosperity and assist you with his hand and heart in adversity." Also, in the meanwhile, through the effort of making that friend you'll have had some fine practice in getting out of the easy rut that runs like a smooth, slick toboggan course straight into old age.

Thinking back over my own relationships, I find that a number of them have come out of activities in which I was involved. During one election I recall working as a volunteer at a local Democratic headquarters and while our candidate came out of the campaign a loser I came out of that same campaign having won two good friends.

Activities are an excellent source of new friends. Almost any activity to which you commit yourself will usually spin off at least one friend.

Always a good source, of course, is your place of work. Water coolers and coffee breaks are rich spawning grounds.

A cousin of mine was called to jury duty and out of that jury came three very good friends of his.

The raw material for friends is everywhere, sometimes on your very block, sometimes in your own apartment house. And often opportunities pop up in most unlikely places. It's just that, unfortunately, the majority of people won't venture the first move, as did my friend Lela. Matter of fact, it was from Lela that I originally learned the beauty of making that first overture.

Quite late one lovely summer night I was out walking when I noticed a group of people clustered on the sidewalk. At the curb was a police car. A couple of policeman had two young men shoved up against the side of the car and were searching them. Fascinated, as are most people, with that sort of melodrama, I stopped. Standing next to me was a man and a woman and shortly we struck up a conversation. We speculated wildly, were the two young men jewel thieves? Or were they perhaps drug addicts or international spies or rapists...? Just as I'd decided that I could no longer bear the suspense and that I must go over and question the policemen they shoved the two young men in the car and drove away. The man and the woman and I stood and chatted for a while, introduced ourselves, then finally with the customary "So very nice to have met you and hope we meet again sometime," went our separate ways.

And in all probability our ways would have remained separate forevermore. "Hope we meet again sometime" would have been the epitaph on that very pleasant encounter if, a few days later, I hadn't received a note from the woman. Lela. She had looked up my address in the telephone book and had taken the trouble to write me, telling me how much both she and her husband had enjoyed meeting me. It would be so nice, she said, if we could have lunch together one day, or perhaps I'd come to dinner.

I was charmed by the gesture. It's customary, I realize, for a man to make the first move toward a woman. Or a woman toward a man, for that matter. As a sex ploy, it's not in the least unusual. But for a woman in a situation such as ours to go out of her way to make the first move toward friendship with another woman is unusual. It's unusual and rare, just as is Lela, I find, now that she has become a close and treasured friend.

There's an interesting statistic that I came across recently which maintains that 2% of people make things happen, 3% watch things happen and the other 95% haven't the faintest idea of what's happening. Among the 2% who make things happen is without doubt the place to be. No question about that. So if you're not already in that elite 2%, make it a point to join now. Make the phone call or write the note if you should stumble onto someone with whom a friendship seems warmly promising. Don't sit back and wait for the other fellow to do it.

It's easier that way, of course. But the chances are 90 to 1 that he belongs to the 3% that watch things happen. And so the chances are 100 to 1 that nothing will happen except that you'll have lost out on a lovely opportunity for a new friend.

Now in this process of building up new friendships you should be aware of the fact that you're likely to be more readily accepted if you give others some bonus along with yourself. Unless you happen to be extraordinary or unusually fascinating offering nothing but your own company is scarcely going to cause new friends to beat down your doors.

This may not be a particularly palatable concept to swallow. You may feel that you would like to be much sought after merely because you're you. And if you're Margaret Thatcher or Woody Allen you will be. But since you're not, toss out some sort of lure: lure meaning, according to the dictionary, that which entices by the prospect of advantage or pleasure.

On a lure scale of one to ten I would rate an invitation to dinner a one. But if it's true that you can't cook (or if you're only utilizing that protestation as an excuse) it's nothing to worry about. There are other perfectly acceptable lures. Just a short distance down the scale, perhaps a three, is dessert and coffee, a few glasses of wine perhaps, a collection of records, other interesting or amusing guests. And of course, if you happen to have an extra ticket to a concert or to the theatre, you've shot up to the top of the scale again, probably to a two.

Then there are other lures you can offer that are not tangible ones. Sometimes just a favor. For instance, an acquaintance of mine telephoned me not long ago. She was a casual acquaintance, our only bond being that we had the same cleaning woman who came to us on different days. Helen wanted to know if I could possibly change days with her. For some reason or other, her regular day was inconvenient. As it happened, changing days for me would have meant switching a couple of appointments and somewhat rearranging my schedule. Politely but firmly I said I was sorry but didn't see how I could manage it.

Helen couldn't have been nicer and more understanding but after I'd hung up I felt vaguely uncomfortable. I realized that by no stretch of the imagination could I be termed friendly or obliging. I could have accommodated Helen. It had just seemed too much bother. And I'd compounded the shabbiness by being inflexible (which in itself was diametrically opposed to my principles).

Quickly I went to the telephone and called her back.

"Helen," I said, "I find I can change days with you after all. Means just a little moving things around and I'd be glad to do it ... No, no, it's not too much trouble for me. Really. What? ... Why, of course I'm a doll—didn't you know?"

A week later Helen invited me to a party she was giving. Having discovered what a doll I was, I suppose she couldn't resist including me as a guest. I discovered that she, too, was a doll. So happily, unwittingly, I made my quota for the year, one new friend. Just through that single small gesture.

Whatever the method you use to gather new friends and from wherever you choose to gather them, there's one category that's particulary important to cultivate. Those are the people who are happily involved in hobbies and interests of various sorts. These people, if they perceive that you're at all interested, will delight in discussing their hobbies with you. Just try saying to one of them, "I understand from Jack (or John or Mabel) that you're starting a vegetable garden. Well, how do you know what will grow in your particular soil?" or "I hear you have a system for winning at blackjack. How does it work?" A single question will as a rule set them off. And before you're through, in all likelihood you'll be invited to join them. I know, in my own case, I'm hooked on aerobic dancing. And if someone so much as asks me a single question about what it is exactly I have him enrolled in the class before he knows quite what struck him.

So you see, in addition to sowing the seeds of a new friendship, you'll probably add a new pursuit to the ones you've already woven into your life. And, too, these people are generally the most alive and the most stimulating people. They're the ones who stay young and who'll give you a leg up toward staying young.

Then, into the melange of friends I cultivate, I always try to toss a dollop or two of those who've chalked up fewer chronological years than I.

With friends, as with all other sectors of my life, you see, I'm preparing ahead. For I've noticed, as perhaps have you, that in later years, your contemporaries often have a habit of dying off before you. This could easily cause you to fall back on the dirge-like lament, "All of my friends are gone," and make almost irresistible the temptation to lay added demands on the unwilling shoulders of your children or your relatives. However, if you're fortunate enough to have included some younger friends in your circle of intimates, the odds are good that they'll be around longer than you, which will make it much easier for you to bypass the big D's—Desperation, Desolation and Despair.

11.

Just last week a friend of mine said to me, "I don't know when I've sat down to read a book. It's been ages!" As a matter of fact, two friends within two days of each other came out with that same remark.

Sorely tempted though I was, I said not a word.

I said not a word either to my television repairman, when on one of his visits, we happened to touch on the subject of reading and he said lightly, "Oh, I never bother to read ... my wife does enough reading for the two of us."

If he hadn't been such a sensational repairman, I would have snapped, "That's a dumb remark if I ever heard one." However, I held my tongue. I couldn't help but think, though, what a grievous pity it was for someone to let a richly rewarding occupation like reading books go by the board, and with such casualness and so little compunction. I remembered suddenly what John Cowper Powys, in his book *The Meaning of Culture*, had to say about reading. "The effects of long absorption in reading," he wrote, "is to purge the mind of petty and annoying thought and leave us amiable, genial and benevolent."

Just those few benefits that accrue to us from reading would be gift enough. But above and beyond the inducements laid out by Mr. Powys are the gems Aldous Huxley strews before us. Huxley said, "Every man who knows how to read has it in his power to magnify himself, to multiply the ways in which he exists, to make his life full, significant and interesting." And there, or course, is the real nub of the statement. For having it within your power to make your life one that is full, significant and interesting gives you the power for a successful standoff with old age.

And yet, despite these many beautiful, life-enhancing pluses, that gradual ceasing to read as the years pass remain, for most peple, all too common. Unless, of course, you take into account the daily newspaper and those superficial magazines baring the sumptuous details of Zsa Zsa Gabor's latest divorce settlement, both of them effortless sorts of reading, demanding little thought and little or no concentration.

"Rest," says an old German proverb, "leads to rust." And, undeniably, this sort of easy, shallow reading can be classified under the heading of rest ... that rest which leads to rust. I'm not attempting to tout you off of your beloved newspaper or your favorite magazine. I recognize that reading the newspaper is a part of life, too. As is "oohing and aahing" over Miss Gabor's latest divorce settlement or the solid gold fittings in her newest Rolls-Royce. I only suggest that you sandwich in some other sort or reading as well—some anti-rust reading.

For instance, there's Clifton Fadiman's Reading Plan. Mr. Fadiman has what he calls a Lifetime Reading Plan that consists of 100 books, any one of which can qualify as an effective rust preventive. Since a few of Mr. Fadiman's prestigious accomplishments include having been general editor of the *New Yorker* magazine, writer and lecturer for the *Encyclopedia Britannica* as well as a teacher of the Great Books course in Chicago, New York and Los Angeles, I felt that his reading plan would be very well worth following. So when the Plan appeared some 20 years back in the local newspaper, I cut it out, with the firm resolve to read through the entire list long before this. Of course I haven't. I was shorn of my resolve by the exigencies of time and, I shamefacedly admit, by inertia. However, I have checked off quite a few of them. And before I check out, I hope to check off all of these fine classics. Please don't shudder. I know that word "classic" often brings on a shudder. But these books are a long way from being dreary tomes. I promise you. In Mr. Fadiman's own words, "These books are there for your *enjoyment*." The underlining is Mr. Fadiman's, not mine. And he goes on to say, "There's nothing solemn about feeling your mind stretch. It's the most rewarding feeling in the world ... These books are an adventure."

Naturally it's impossible to list here the entire hundred. What I have done is to excerpt from Mr. Fadiman's hundred a small sprinkling. And, out of that sprinkling, you in turn may choose your own sprinkling which cannot help but be a splendid jumping-off place toward making your life, in Mr. Huxley's words, more "full, significant, and interesting."

Mr. Fadiman's Lifetime Reading Plan is broken up into eight sections. They're headed Plays, Poetry, Some Early Greeks, History and Biography, etc. I've selected the section headed Narrative, primarily because of Mr. Fadiman's own comment regarding this particular list. He writes, "These wonderful stories are interesting not only because they are entertaining but because they often contain more life-wisdom than the profoundest philosophy." An irresistible combination, it seemed to me, entertainment plus life-wisdom.

There are 33 books under this heading from which I have chosen 10. My choice was a purely arbitrary one and, I might add, a most difficult one.

The books are:

Gulliver's Travels	by Jonathan Swift
Wuthering Heights	by Emily Bronte
Lord Jim	by Joseph Conrad
David Copperfield	by Charles Dickens
Alice in Wonderland	by Lewis Carroll
Candide	by Voltaire
The Magic Mountain	by Thomas Mann
Don Quixote	by Cervantes
Madame Bovary	by Flaubert
Robinson Crusoe	by Daniel Defoe

Some of you may be familiar with the lot of them but for those of you who aren't you'll find whichever one you choose as a beginning, a worthy launching pad. What's more, they're all in the Public Library, so they'll cost you even less than your daily newspaper.

If, by now, you've really been thoroughly seduced by the idea of anti-rust reading but are somewhat intimidated by the word "classic" don't back off from the whole idea and throw away the baby with the bath water. There are other ways to go. For instance, one good way is to take out a membership in the Book-of-the-Month club. They are not classics but they're books that are very worthwhile. Incidentally, joining the club is a fine and a forceful technique for cultivating the habit of reading. You agree to purchase four books a year, at a reduced rate, and since no one I've ever encountered relishes the idea of throwing away money, chances are you're going to read the books. In case the Book-of-the-Month holds enough of an appeal that you're impelled to join, or at least to write in and get more detailed information, their address is Camp Hill, Pennsylvania 17012.

The Literary Guild operates along somewhat the same lines. So it, too, is a prod toward reading. The address there Dept. WR 243, Garden City, N.Y. 11530.

For paperbacks, try the Quality Paperback Book club, whose slogan, incidentally, is "The first book club for smart people who aren't rich." In QPB, the requirement is that you buy only one paperback every six months, and, of course, at a considerable discount. Their address is Middletown, Pennsylvania 17057.

Whatever method you opt for, the library, one of the book clubs, the Lifetime Reading Plan, or perhaps a skillful combination of several, is not of great moment. What's important is that you get into the habit of some anti-rust reading and that you stick with it for the duration of what will become your "full, significant and interesting" lifetime.

"But even if I don't read all that much," some women might protest, "my brain is in no danger of rusting out. Because I do think! I have to think—about what to fix for dinner, about the kids' clothes, about our social life..."

And some of you men might be equally defensive. "I think about my job, about the work I do, I'd get fired the hell out of there if I didn't. And I think about my family and their needs..."

All essential thinking, of course. But scarcely the brand of thinking that broadens your horizons, that breaks up your mental adhesions, that keeps you from getting old.

I was at a spa in Palm Springs recently, up to my earlobes in hot mineral water when I overheard a woman discussing her family with another woman. She was telling the other woman how brilliant all of them were. Her husband, she said, was a psychiatric social worker and her daughter and her son were each, respectively, studying social science and psychology.

"And My God, you should hear them at the dinner table when they all get together!" she said. "They yak and yak about all that stuff, so I just get up and go out in the kitchen and make coffee."

Despite herself, this woman was being exposed to exciting ideas and thoughts that were new to her. She was being presented with a perfect, ready-made opportunity to expand her horizons. And what did she do with it? She went out into the kitchen and made coffee.

However, had Thomas Edison been splashing around in that hot mineral water, I'm sure he wouldn't have been in the least taken aback by the woman's reaction. For it was he who said, "There is no expediency to which man will not resort to avoid the real labor of thinking."

And Bertrand Russell, if he'd been alongside me in the pool, might very well have cried out triumphantly, "You see, that only proves what a damn smart cookie I am!" His famous and wry comment on the subject of thinking was, "Most people would die sooner than think. In fact, they do so."

And he *was* a damn smart cookie. You do die. In the words of the singer, Bob Dylan, "If you ain't busy livin', you're busy dyin'." Not all at once, of course. When you stagnate, you die bit by bit. Until there comes the time when you're not alive at all any more. Not really alive. Oh, your organs may be functioning. A man I know once said to me, "I have a good appetite, that's half of living. And every day I have a good cigar, that's the other half." So in a very primitive respect he was alive. But not when you consider one of Mr. Webster's definitions of the word alive, which in my opinion is the definitive one. According to his definition the word alive means, "To live a life rich in experience, to live vigorously in respect to thought, activity or emotions."

Incidentally, that's a very good technique to employ when you want to make a check on whether you're really alive or not. Ask yourself the question, "Am I living a life high in experience? Am I living vigorously in respect to thought, activity or emotion?"

It's a much more accurate way to check on yourself than the way in which my friend Pearl River does it. Pearl is a lady in her 70's and this is how she checks on whether she's alive or not.

I wake up each morning and dust off my wits
Then I reach for the paper and read the obits,
If my name's not among 'em I know I'm not dead!
So I eat a big breakfast and hop back into bed.

Pearl River is surely not dead. But she's just as surely not alive, obituaries notwithstanding. How about you?

How much thinking do you do about things with which you're unfamiliar? How many times, when you run across a word you've never encountered before, in print or in conversation, do you go directly to the dictionary to look it up, then proceed to make a note of its derivation and incorporate it indelibly into your vocabulary? When you hear time-worn phrases such as "He's happy as a clam," or "You have to take that with a grain of salt," do you ever pause to speculate on their origins, on what exactly they mean, how they came into being a part of the language? How many times a month do you make it a point to take part in a thought-provoking discussion from which you emerge with a new viewpoint, or which propels you along a new avenue of thinking? And when, on occasion, you're exposed to an idea that's new to you, do you, like the lady in the Palm Springs spa, go out in the kitchen and make coffee, or do you sit tight and listen? And listen intently. Then perhaps go on from there and do some reading on the subject so that the next time you might even be knowledgeable enough to make some small contribution?

Some of you may feel of course that you don't want to be bothered with such a lot of strenuous thinking. I've heard people say, "Oh, I'm alive enough for all practical purposes. I'm not worried."

However, before you hand down a summary dismissal such as that, it's well to bear in mind the fact that nature is harsh and uncompromising in the penalties she exacts for not keeping fully alive, for letting your mind sit and stew in its same stale juices.

And one of her more severe penalties is forgetfulness.

It's not necessarily because of age that we become forgetful, although that's the conclusion we generally hug to our hearts. You've all known children who were very forgetful. And why? Because they're not paying attention. Because they're only half listening.

That's one of the most common reasons for forgetfulness—going through life not bothering to give it your full and rapt attention, only half-hearing, half-seeing, being only half-alive. As Emerson puts it, "We live all our life with our eyelids heavy with sleep."

Dr. Lillian Martin, founder of the Old Age Counselling Center in San Francisco, insists that people of any age can rehabilitate, even restore, their memories, by training themselves in attention and recall.

One exercise in training yourself in attention and recall is, I think, of special value to cultivate. You'll find it an exercise that's not only effective as an aid to your memory but it's effective as well in saving you time and aggravation. If, when you put something away or just lay something down, you pause for only a moment and rivet your full and entire attention on exactly where you're putting it away or where you're laying it down, you'll find that when you come back to look for it you won't have to scurry around frantically, wondering where the blasted thing's hiding. You'll remember where the blasted thing's hiding. Because of that one moment of strict and complete attention you gave to the object when you put it down. It's quite a simple technique but what the unflagging practice of it accomplishes is to outlaw gradually that habit of only half-hearing, only half-seeing, being only half-alive, to which we're all so disastrously addicted.

One other very common reason for forgetfulness is that we haven't taken the trouble to feed our minds constantly. We've failed to supply them with fresh ammunition: fresh new thoughts, fresh new ideas. And the intellect can be aptly compared to an oil lamp. Unless you keep it regularly filled, it dies out as time passes.

It's been said that the true age of a person can be measured by the degree of pain he or she feels as they come into contact with a new thought or a new idea. If that is so, and I believe stoutly that it is, then it might be a wise move for you to start chalking up your measurements.

We're magnificent, we human beings. And it's painfully sad and depressing when you consider that most of us barely use ourselves. It's rather like owning a priceless grand piano and playing nothing on it but "Chopsticks."

However, happily, there is a choice. And, as always, that choice is yours. You can bang out only "Chopsticks" on your priceless piano and get old. Or you can commit yourself irrevocably to staying young and make that piano sing with some of the loveliest arias ever flung into the ether.

12.

There are three bugaboos in particular that are very widespread, and that it would behoove you to keep a sharp eye out for it if you're desirous of blockading the road that leads to getting old. All of these three have a way of sneaking up on you with silent footsteps as the years roll by.

The first one of the three is self-centeredness.

This trait I lump in the same category with bad breath. They're both on the offensive side; they both tend to cause people to avoid you; and there is scarcely a soul intrepid enough to call either of them to your attention.

I have an aunt who's become very self-centered with the years and now that she's not too well it's particularly exaggerated. I dropped in to see her not long ago and the conversation we had was typical of conversations with the self-centered old. I started to tell her about plans for the promotion of my forthcoming book. I went into quite a little detail because I thought it would be of interest to her and would liven up her day

After I'd talked for just a few minutes, I paused, expecting some question or comment about the book. Her comment was, "You know what? I've found the most wonderful new doctor! He gives you his entire attention. And he's so thorough. Last week I was in his office for a checkup and he gave me the most exhaustive one, inside and out. Oh—" she flicked a triumphant wrist at me—"guess what he told me? He said I had the internal organs of a girl of 26!" Of course I couldn't understand why that was such splendid news. They don't show anyhow. But I said nothing. I was forced to say nothing since she was going on and on about the new doctor.

Well, I have what I consider a surefire technique to head off this sort of self-absorption. I ran across it in a comedy I read once. The lead in this play was a very successful and attractive career woman but she seemed to have no luck whatsoever with men. Her grandmother, who was a very wise old lady, told her not to be so bright with men, as a matter of fact, not to say anything at all to them except for three words: (with delighted surprise) "Yes?" (with delighted incredulity) "No!" (with delighted interest) "Really?"

Of course in the play, which was very amusing, the girl followed her grandmother's admonition to the letter and wound up with an absolutely peerless man.

I thought that grandmother's advice was excellent advice, an excellent technique that all of us can use to good advantage, not necessarily in snaring a man (though I've found it works there, too, like a charm) but in our everyday contacts. Because when you're using just those three words, "Yes?" "No!" "Really?" or a facsimile thereof, it's a virtual impossibility to go on about yourself. You just cannot be self-centered. You're compelled to listen to the other person.

And the results of utilizing this technique are sometimes quite unexpected. I was in a coffee shop one noontime having lunch. Sitting at the counter next to me was a very pleasant man and, as often happens at counters, we started to talk. We chatted for perhaps half an hour and when I rose to leave he said, "I don't know when I've enjoyed a conversation as much as this one. You're the most interesting woman." And actually all I'd done the entire time was quietly eat my egg salad sandwich and say occasionally, between bites, "Yes?" "No!" "Really?"

Try it once just for fun. But not only once. Adopt those three words into your vocabulary. And use them often enough so that they become an integral part of your thinking. At times you'll have to vary the formula, perhaps change the words to fit the conversation. You can be as creative as you please so long as you stay with the basic technique. Because the practice of that technique is a superb method for becoming other-centered, for putting a stop to the glaringly self-involved garrulousness that can so frequently overtake you with the years and will so successfully make you old.

The second of the three bugaboos that mark old age is

touchiness. I'm sure many of you have encountered this quick touchiness in old people. You've undoubtedly discovered how easily hurt many of them are. That oversensitivity to slights, and often to what are in reality only imagined slights, seems to be one of the bleaker characteristics of age. Why this should be so—why this oversensitivity is so frequently a hallmark of age is really quite easy to understand when you take into account the lives led by most people we term old, lives that are so empty and fruitless that every event, every remark takes on an importance far beyond its due. But whatever the reason behind this trait is really not of great consequence. What does matter is your awareness of the tendency when you catch the very first glimpse of it in yourself; and if and when that happens, that you have in your possession the tools to scotch the tendency before it becomes full-blown.

An excellent technique to accomplish this is to make it a habit, early in life, to refuse to interpret things that are said or done to you as personal insults. Realize that people are not sitting and diabolically plotting to make you the butt of their anger, or their rage, or even of their indifference. They are not deliberately attempting to "do you in." In the words of the novelist, Laura Huxley, "You are not the target."

If, for instance, in traffic, a pedestrian shouts at you or, as seems to be the fashion these days, makes an obscene gesture in your direction, when all you've done is gently tap your horn in an attempt to spare him a broken arm or leg, remember that you are not necessarily the target. He may be worried about his job or his wife in the hospital or how he's going to pay for the braces on his kids' teeth. Chances are he's beleaguered by all the pressures of living and that he hasn't yelled specifically at you. Of course he has no right to take out his frustrations on you! I couldn't agree more. But there's little you can do about him. The only thing you can do, with profit, is to remind yourself doggedly that you are not the target.

And if a salesperson gives you the glassy-eyed, indifferent treatment when you're taking a little extra time to make up your mind about a shirt, remember that he may be hating his job or being vastly underpaid or nursing a hangover worthy of entry in the *Guinness Book of Records*. I don't say for one minute that that situation is a particularly appetizing one to

73

be caught in. I know. I've been caught in it myself. Go ahead and speak up if you will. Just remember, though, that YOU ARE NOT THE TARGET.

Josh Billings, the American humorist, once said, "The best creed we can have is charity toward the creeds of others." So accustom yourself to be forbearing, to be tolerant of the vagaries of others. That is, if you want to hang on to your youthful way of thinking, if you're determined to avoid the touchiness of the old. It will make it somewhat easier for you if you manage to bear in mind that all of us have different, and in some cases even quite odd, ways of behaving.

Perhaps you don't. Perhaps you're completely free of any peculiarities. Check it out, though, just in case. I know as far as I'm concerned, I wouldn't have the temerity to be smug or critical or scornful of anyone else's craziness when I think of my coat.

I have a very old, very shabby tweed coat that I drape over my bed, on top of the rest of my covers, each night. The lining is in shreds, the buttons are all missing, but its lightness and its warmth are just exactly right and I love it dearly. If there's ever a fire in my house and firemen come bursting in to rescue me I'm sure I'd die. Not of the flames or the fumes, but of shame. Because there would be that shabby, ragged coat in full view. Of course, I keep it carefully hidden in my closet during the day. But when night falls, out it comes. I haven't quite gotten around to taking it with me when I travel. However, I must admit that I miss it.

Every now and then when my sister comes to my house she spots the coat. "Eve!" she'll cry, "why don't you throw that miserable thing away? It's a disgrace."

But you see, I can't afford to throw it away. It's not just that it serves to keep me warm and cozy, but it serves to build my forbearance. It forces me to be tolerant of the other fellow's viewpoint, of whatever quirks he may happen to have in his collection, and so it serves to keep me young.

The third of the three bugaboos to keep a vigilant eye out for is self-pity.

I think you'll agree that self-pity is one of the more unattractive traits around. "Poor me" for this reason, or "Poor me" for that reason, or for any reason whatsoever, is certainly not calculated to win hearts. When I encounter it face to face, it always provokes a desperate desire for a quick getaway. And I'm willing to wager that I'm not alone in that reaction.

But whatever the effect on others it's not nearly so tragic as the effect of self-pity on the victim. When a person, of any age, is thrown back upon an attitude of pity for himself, he loses completely the joyous ability to like himself and, concomitantly, to enjoy himself. To wend one's way through life bearing that burden is a very costly price to pay for whatever satisfaction trickles from the role of self-pitier.

Only last week I found a friend of mine buried under a landslide of self-pity when I happened to telephone her.

"You know," Jean said, "I've been in bed with the flu for over a week and I didn't hear word one from any of my friends."

It was no feat of ESP to sense the accusatory note in her voice.

"Oh, I'm sorry to hear you were ill," I said. "I didn't have the slightest idea or I certainly would have called."

The small tinge of sarcasm was unmistakable when she replied, "I would have appreciated that."

"But Jean, how could I have known?"

"Well," she said reluctantly, "I suppose you couldn't."

"As a matter of fact, there's been a virtual epidemic of the flu. Almost everyone around has been laid low."

"It doesn't help much to know that."

"I only mentioned it because that's probably the reason you didn't hear from anyone...Feeling okay now?"

"Not quite, but much better."

"Well, cheer up, baby," I said lightly. "I'll be over tomorrow, loaded with red carnations. They're your favorites, I know. So stay alive and you can enjoy them...but if you're dead, don't worry, they'll be terrific at your funeral! How's that for covering all bases?"

Jean retorted sharply, "That's not funny."

I should have known better. In my experience, I've discovered that the people who are most likely to fall prey to self-pity are almost inevitably those who are lacking a sense of humor. And I must say, Jean was never noted for her sense of humor.

Now by sense of humor I don't mean wit nor do I mean the ability to crack jokes. I mean it in the sense that Webster phrases it in one of his definitions. He says, "To adjust matters to the exigencies of, to adapt oneself to." In other words, to accept your situation, whatever it may be, and in a lighthearted manner.

I knew a man who exemplified perfectly the sense of humor that Webster describes. This man was a lifelong student of philosophy and when he was 50 he developed gout which gave him a great deal of pain. He never ever referred to it, except once, when he said to me, "You know, my philosophy has reconciled me to a great many things. Even to gout." His eyes twinkled as he added, "But gout only in other people."

The father of a good friend of mine exhibited an equally delicious sense of humor. He was in his eighties and in remarkably good health except for his memory. That he'd made no attempt to work on rehabilitating and it was by now practically nonexistent. But not for a moment did he bemoan the fact nor did he expect any sympathy. He was completely lighthearted about it. He once said, "I'm just as strong as I ever was. I can work just as hard as any young fella. Of course my mind's all gone," with a shrug, "but I don't miss it any!"

And one last beautiful example of this sort of humor is the remark made by an aging lady to her daughter. "You know," she said cheerily, "so many of my friends complain that they're bored. The days drag for them, they say. But you see, they're not as lucky as I am. I spend three minutes out of every five dropping, losing or misplacing things. That leaves me only two minutes to get things done. So my days just whizz by!"

That sense of humor about yourself, that lighthearted manner about your plight, whatever it may be, are not qualities native to everyone. But if you're not one of the blessed ones, I'm sure it will be comforting to know that they can be developed. I'll admit it takes quite a lot of thought and quite a bit of effort along the way. But I must reiterate, they can be developed. Giving the thought and making the effort to develop this brand of humor, then keeping it highly polished and active through constant usage is almost, if not equally, as important to your life as maintaining a top level of health and building a comfortable level of money in your bank account.

13.

Among the people who tend to indulge in self-pity is one particular group that is especially prone to it. These are the parents who never gave any thought in their younger days to the proper parent-child relationship, the parents who, unfortunately, put all their stakes in their children, who lived only for and through those children.

And in the lives of those parents there is one day that is generally an exceedingly traumatic one. That day is their child's twenty-first birthday.

By the time this birthday rolls around the strings between parent and child should be cut, for the happiness of both. The child is now the potential parent. He is soon to find another family, one of his own, on whom to lavish his love and affection. Or if not another family, at least a roof-tree of his own to absorb him. But the parent who has sunk all of his stakes in that child is going to experience endless difficulty and a great deal of pain pulling those stakes up and letting his child go.

Now I'm not advocating that children drop their parents into the limbo of the past. I'm addressing myself to the parents. Your children will continue loving and respecting you, if they did as they were growing up, with one exception; if they're made to feel that they owe it to you, for all your sacrifices, to give up any part of their lives in return. That is bound to fill them with the seeds of resentment. And if you should, by any chance, remind them in subtle, and sometimes not so subtle, ways that they are not giving you, as a parent, what you consider your full due, then there's almost sure to be a full-scale rebellion. And you will be not only miserably unhappy but awash in self-pity as well.

Unfortunately, self-pity has a disastrous way of rushing to the head and then pouring out of the mouth on a tide of reproach. So that if your children come by on an all too infrequent visit, you're quite likely to spew forth, "You haven't been here in weeks, you know," and then, because the tide is so strong, "And you haven't even called!" BUT DON'T SAY IT. No matter how sorely tempted you are, DON'T SAY IT. No matter that you're right, DON'T SAY IT.

And when they're getting ready to leave, if it seems practically irresistible to ask, "Oh, do you *have* to go so soon?" or "When am I going to see you again?" RESIST. With the entire collection of fibers in your being. Questions like that won't do one iota of good. They won't suceed in making them stay longer or come back any sooner. What it will succeed in doing is make them feel pressured and guilty.

Substitute instead words like, "I'm so pleased that you came. I enjoyed being with you so much, " or "I'll be looking forward to seeing you again whenever you can make it." And say it without the tiniest trace of a whimper in your voice, or in your eyes. Your reward will be worth it, I guarantee you ... the reward of seeing the look of relief and pleasure on their faces or the extra warmth of the hug you'll earn.

If it seems to demand more strength than you can dredge up to give them a greeting and a send-off like that just keep in mind one fact that may be unwelcome but nonetheless true: they owe you nothing. You had your fun in raising them. Or if you didn't, it's no fault of theirs. In actuality, it's you who owe them something. Make them aware that you realize you no longer hold the strings, that from now on they move completely under their own power. And for the sake of your own ease of heart and spirit, realize at the same time that moving under their own power can very possibly mean that they won't move often in your direction.

If you're sufficiently wise to give thought to this, wise enough to prepare for this day well ahead of time, you won't feel that you've lost your children because they're engrossed in their own lives.

And what's most important, you won't feel woefully neglected and engulfed in self-pity.

I knew of a woman who had a complete breakdown because

she'd lived only for and through her children and when they were grown they showed her, as she put it, "No consideration at all." So her life was shattered.

It's well to remember that respect and consideration do not have to be demanded by those who have prepared properly. Usually it's cheerfully given. But if, by some chance, it's not, and if you've prepared ahead of time, at least you'll survive. Your life won't splinter into a mass of shards.

There is, of course, a very good technique that I recomend if your children are remiss in their attentions to you. It's a technique that's highly popular and most effective in political circles. And it's equally as effective, you'll find, in your own small personal circle. It's called bribery. It's first cousin to the "luring" technique that I so highly advocated using with friends.

A top-notch form of bribery, for instance, is to invite your children for dinner, making sure to cook something that's one of their all-time favorites. Make sure, too, that when you issue the invitation you inform them of the upcoming menu. Then from the time the door of your house or apartment opens for them until it closes behind them, don't complain, about anything. And, no matter how strong the provocation, don't criticize. Keep the flow of conversation as lively and as entertaining as possible and preferably concentrated on them and their activities. Oh, you can toss in a minor amount of talk about your own activities. Knowing that you're involved in a life of your own will please them. It lifts from them any small burden of guilt they may be shouldering about their relationship with you.

Then, when they leave, if you're financially able, tuck a small check obtrusively into one of their pockets. That is, unless they happen to be much richer than you, in which event, hold up the check.

Offering to babysit with the grandchildren is another first-rate form of bribery. This one has several worthwhile fringe benefits, too. Your children will have to bring their kids over and later on pick them up, which gives you two chances of seeing them. In addition, you'll be earning points for giving them the freedom to gallivant. And, as a choice added bonus, you'll have some time to spend with your grandchildren.

I have a friend who's a clinical psychologist. He has a good relationship with his daughter, but it's considerably enhanced by the fact that whenever the daughter has any sort of trouble, in her domestic life, on her job, with her children, she knows her father can be counted on for wise and expert counselling. Even his grandchildren turn to him eagerly for help with their teenage problems. His is a somewhat more subtle form of bribery, but it's bribery nonetheless.

I rarely get to see my beloved young grandniece except when she needs help with a paper she's been assigned to write for her English class. Then she telephones me and asks to come by. It's just lucky for me that I happen to be a writer or I'd probably see her not at all. It would be quite easy for me to wallow in self-pity. Instead I resort to bribery. The help I give her and which I shamelessly encourage her to seek from me is, although she is unaware of it, my way of doing just that. It usually results in her getting an "A" paper. Naturally this delights her. But it pleases me almost as much because I'm afraid that the day may come when our combined talents will net her only a B- or even a C. On that day my sly bribery will have lost its shimmer and my grandniece's visits will almost certainly come to a halt.

I must say I have run into a great deal of indignation from many parents on this technique of bribery.

"If my children have to be bribed to come to see me," they cry, "they can stay away!"

"I wouldn't dream of stooping to such measures!"

"I'm not going to knock myself out to get them to visit me! Not a chance."

Well, all I have to say in rebuttal is, "I would certainly knock myself out to get them to come to see me," (if you choose to call it knocking yourself out.) And "I would dream of stooping to any measures," (if you choose to consider it stooping.) I not only would, but I do. I don't hesitate for one second to bribe my grandniece, in any way I can, if it results in my getting to see her more often.

Bribery, in this sense, is not a dirty word. It only means injecting pleasurable gratification into what is, more often than not, dutiful obligation. What a lovely feeling to know that never again in your childrens' house will be heard the words,

"We really ought to go see my parents."

One of Machiavelli's more famous lines is, "The means justifies the end." Since you must agree that seeing your children is a good end, start now utilizing the technique of bribery. And I think you'll discover that you've spawned a troupe of bribees who, at the prospect of paying you a visit, will begin to glow instead of grouse.

14.

In the magazine *U.S. News and World Report*, I ran across a charming letter from a woman who wrote; "In the last issue of *U.S. News and World Report* I found the following about activity, age, etc., 'Short naps after lunch and before dinner are a very good idea when you reach middle age. At age 50 take a half day off in midweek. At age 55 two half days. At age 60 three half days.' Now about my husband. He is nearly ninety. He goes to his office every day, leaving home about 9:20 in the morning. At noon he goes to his club for about an hour and a half, then back to the office and I call for him at 4:30. He doesn't take any naps. He does exercises that he learned 70 years ago at the Y.M.C.A. He plays golf, and I can't do anything with him to make him stop some of these things. He just laughs at me. He had a semiannual checkup a few days ago and he said the doctor can't find a thing the matter with him. Now what am I going to do with this man?"

For openers, I think this concerned lady had better get rid of that energetic young husband and find herself an older man!

Some of you might say, "Well, he's unusual. At 90 most people don't have that kind of energy." True, undoubtedly, but many people don't have that kind of energy at 70 or 60 or even at 50. Energy, it appears, has a most tenuous connection with the number of years a person has lived. I think the observation about energy made by the noted psychologist and philosopher, William James, hits much closer to the mark. He said, "Excitement, ideas and efforts are what give energy." And he might have added, "and are what keep you young." So, barring any real medical problem, if you happen to be one of those whose energy is chronically at low ebb, I urge you strongly to tack up on your private bulletin board that unequivocal statement by William James.

If you'll notice, Mr. James doesn't make mention of any new breakfast food or any fancy medical compound that will infuse you with energy. Vitamin B complex is helpful to someone who is suffering from a deficiency of B, iron can be most helpful in anemia, and I'm certainly in favor of everyone ingesting plenty of protein, vitamins and minerals. But, unfortunately, they won't create a productive daily program or present you with goals that are worth striving for and that will generate excitement, ideas and efforts.

I would hazard a guess that the bustling husband with the very concerned wife was alight with enthusiasm about his work and hence enjoyed going daily to his office. In addition, I would make a hefty wager that he was especially fitted for whatever the work in which he was engaged. I've noticed that people who are in a line of endeavor for which they're ideally suited in general have an abundance of energy. It follows naturally. For excitement, ideas and effort come easily and plentifully when you're in a niche that is consonant with your characteristics and capabilities.

I have a nephew who's a manufacturer's representative who falls into that category. We call him Robert the Mint, because he makes nothing but money. Bob has enormous charm, he handles people exceedingly well, he entertains his customers lavishly and happily. He also has fresh and unusual notions about building his business (ideas), a capacity for working tirelessly and with relish (efforts) and an enthusiasm for the business that emanates from him like an electric current. In short, he has all the characteristics of a top-notch salesman and so fits perfectly into the slot he's chosen for himself. It's not at all surprising that he's highly successful and that he's the fortunate possessor of unlimited energy.

Of course my nephew is a relatively young man. But chronological years, it would seem, are a negligible factor. The well-known financier Bernard Baruch used to tell a story of his uncle who, at 82, decided to retire. He sold his business, then seeing it do badly in the hands of others he bought it back at the age of eighty-seven over the protests of his family. At 99 he had tripled his assets.

Both of these men, my nephew and Bernard Baruch's uncle, although widely disparate in age and undoubtedly in other areas as well, had one important thing in common. They were both in the exact niche where they belonged. And as a result they both reaped a bounteous harvest of benefits.

If the niche you've selected for yourself isn't a happy, rewarding one, if its edges are jagged and bruising, if it makes you edgy with discomfort or exhausts you with boredom, then hop out. Find yourself a more felicitous niche.

It's not always easy, I'll admit. It takes money and courage. But the penalty for remaining unhappily where you are can be a disastrous one. When you possess an innate aptitude that you're not utilizing, it can result in an interior restlessness and nervousness varying all the way from an inability merely to sit quietly and be content to a heart attack or a total crackup. So hop, if your business or your job or your profession is seriously unsatisfying to you. Having two, or more, careers in a lifetime has become, in these times, acceptable, even somewhat commonplace.

Exactly where to hop to is sometimes a problem. I know in my own case, after I found that writing television scripts was no longer rewarding or pleasurable, it took me over a year of searching to find a new niche. I finally settled on the profession of lecturing, a niche into which I snuggled quite profitably and joyfully for over a decade.

Some years back in the local newspaper there were several pages devoted to stories of men and women who had, in their forties and fifties, changed life styles. I was struck by the story of one man who had been a policeman and was now an artist, painting and selling his pictures. Another man who had been an advertising executive making $60,000 a year was now running a small hotel that he and his wife had bought in New England. Although their income was considerably less, they both said they were infinitely happier. Still another man had given up an administrative post and became a dock worker. Very soon, because of his obvious efficiency, the powers-to-be wanted to promote him to dock manager. But he refused the promotion. He said he didn't want responsibility any more. He was happy with the physical labor of loading and unloading cargo.

These men obviously had had no trouble discovering a new niche for themselves. But everyone's not so fortunate and if you happen to be troubled by a where-to-hop problem, consider taking an aptitude test or (as the University of California at Los Angeles insists firmly on calling it) an interest test. Rather than just aptitudes, the interest test uncovers what you would really like to do. The cost of the test plus several sessions of counselling afterwards is usually reasonable.

Take advantage of it. It could catapult you into a new career; it could toss you into a really felicitous niche where ideas and efforts would begin, as Sir Walter Scott puts it, "gaily to burgeon and broadly to grow."

The manager of a large apartment house, who is a friend of mine, told me that a man of 91 had just moved into one of her apartments and had asked for a five-year lease. A little dubious, she had said to him, "You want—a five-year lease?"

Reassuringly he patted her on the shoulder. "Now don't you worry about that lease. I'm not going to die. Not for a helluva long time. I've got too many things I want to do first to pull a kids' stunt like that."

And with that astonishingly energetic attitude I have no doubt that he's right. He won't die. Not a least "for a helluva long time." Why should he? He's certainly not old.

To be ever interested in the possibilities of one's future is a major youthful trait. And it's absolutely essential because it's basic to the life process. Whenever you lose interest in setting up goals, both long range and near, and give up the exciting, stimulating struggle for the achievement of those goals, that is to grow old, regardless of the age at which it occurs.

I'm sure many of you have experienced the surge of energy that's generated by the expenditure of even some minor effort you've made. I know I have. As I mentioned earlier, I'm happily involved in aerobic dancing. However, on occasion I've found myself tired and unwilling to attend the class. But the course is all paid for in advance and since I hang my hat on the rack with those who loathe being short-changed I harangue myself for a while and then go on over. After I've leaped and danced for 15 or 20 minutes, learning the new steps and polishing the old ones, I find that my fatigue has somehow mysteriously vanished. It isn't really mysterious though when you recall William James' statement: "Excitement, ideas and efforts are what generate energy." And of course the more excitement you feel, the more ideas you carry through, and the more efforts you make, the more energy you tap into.

And the more youth, in the true sense of the word.

Almost as important as the generation of energy is its conservation.

I read a report in the journal of the American Medical Womens' Association of a symposium on the pathology and hygiene of housework that had been held at a congress of the Medical Womens' International Association. This was somewhat of a milestone as it was the very first time that the subject of housework had ever been considered at a medical congress.

Conservation of the housewives' energy was the theme of the symposium. Physicians from several countries emphasized the value of proper methods of sitting, standing, stooping, lifting and carrying. It was noted how helpful it was to organize housework so that light and heavy tasks were alternated. Well-designed kitchens, with sinks and tables of such a height that it would not be necessary for the housewife to stoop, as well as the use of mops and polishers with handles that make kneeling and stooping unnecessary, all were given a prominent place.

Many other valuable hints for housewives were mentioned. For instance, try sitting down to do more of your household tasks, such as peeling potatoes, polishing silver, ironing shirts. There are posture chairs on the market that give support to the upper lumbar and lower thoracic portions of the spine, thus making it impossible for you to slouch as you sit. So in spite of yourself you'll stave off that "poor aching back."

If you must stand, they advised, don't stand with stiff knees, rounded shoulders and curving back, giving a good imitation of a question mark. Instead make sure that your knees are bent a little and relaxed, letting the thighs carry some of the weight of your body. And when you stoop you can again head off the "poor aching back" if you bend your knees and squat, keeping your back straight. This is imperative when you pick up something from the floor, whether it be a howling baby, a drunken husband or just a stray cooking spoon.

There's one other salient point that was stressed in the symposium and I endorse it unqualifiedly. As an indispensable hedge against aging. That is the value of a tranquil mind.

To help achieve that tranquility of mind I suggest that you carve, not ten, but just three commandments onto your personal tablet of stone.

The first one is: Don't work against the pressure of time. Plan your day so that it won't be overcrowded. I realize that for many people that's not easy. And sometimes it may seem virtually impossible. But it's not, actually, if you only sit down and divide the tasks that must be done into two categories: the absolutely essential and the not-quite-so-essential. Then leave the not-quite-so-essential ones until the next day.

"But," comes the anguished cry, "they're *all* essential!"

Not true. I know, from my own experience, that if you're willing to give it a little painstaking thought you'll be able to find some few that you can drop into the not-quite-so-essential category. Certainly if the president of a railroad can do it, you can. The uncle of a friend of mine used to be president of the Philadelphia Railroad, and my friend told me that whenever anyone came in to talk to his uncle, he never failed to find time for a pleasant, unhurried interview. Very impressed with this, my friend, who was just starting out in the business world himself, asked him how, with his heavy responsibilities, he managed it.

His uncle smiled at him. "Well, I like it that way. So I manage to arrange it that way."

My friend, who is himself an executive in a television network by now, handles his own interviews in exactly the same manner. "What my uncle said impressed me so," he told me, "that I learned how I could arrange it. And I have."

So you see, if you like it that way, it can be arranged that way.

The second commandment is: Always allow yourself a little cushion of time for things that need to be done. If, for example, you're due to meet a plane and the trip to the airport takes half an hour, give yourself 45 or even 50 minutes. With that leeway, you'll avoid the throbbing headache or the nervous upset if you happen to be caught in an unexpected traffic jam. Then, if it's going to push you to get to the cleaners to pick up a dress that you've set your heart on wearing to some shindig that night, don't go to the cleaners. Goof off for a while instead and wear something that's hanging in your closet. No one at the party is going to notice your dress. They'll notice rather how fresh and rested you look. And how young.

The third commandment is: Cultivate the habit of relaxing for a short while at least once or twice during the day. There are many stray moments that you can alchemize into golden relaxation opportunities: sitting in buses, in trains, in airplanes, waiting in the doctor's office, the dentist's office, the beauty parlor and also while you wait for members of the family who are late to dinner. Instead of fuming about the dinner spoiling (which it's going to do whether you fume or not) embrace that chance to relax in an easy chair, perhaps with your favorite whodunit, if it will help banish the fuming.

I remember an English character actress named Mary Forbes. I knew that Miss Forbes was not young, chronologically, but she was one of the most astonishingly youthful-looking women I think I have ever met. When I was working as a writer at Metro Goldwyn Mayer studios I wandered down to a sound stage one afternoon to get away from my desk for a while.

Over in a darkened, out of the way corner, I noticed Mary Forbes. She was sitting in an easy chair, her head resting against the back of the chair, her eyes closed. Suddenly the assistant director called out, "Everyone on the set, please." Mary Forbes stood up, ran a hand over her hair, walked out onto the set and played her scene.

As I watched her, I realized that in all probability her lovely, unlined skin was due largely to the softly damp climate of her native England. But England could take no credit for her youthful walk and voice and manner. For those, only Mary Forbes deserved credit.

Later we had an opportunity to chat for a few minutes and in the course of those few minutes she mentioned that one of the habits she'd acquired very early in her career was relaxing completely for five or ten minutes every time she had the chance. Right then and there I decided that I would purloin that habit of Miss Forbes' and make it my own. And so I did. And it has now become my third commandment. I think you'll find, as I did, that firmly abiding by it will pay off handsomely in youth and energy.

As I walked off the set at Metro Goldwyn Mayer that long-ago day, I turned for another look at Mary Forbes. She waved to me and there flashed into my mind a line I'd once heard that seemed at the moment to be particularly apt: "Beautiful young people are a creation of nature. Beautiful old people create themselves."

15.

While blissfully disco dancing a few weeks ago, in almost nonexistent but terribly sexy sandals, I pulled a ligament in my leg. The very first remark out of the mouth of a friend of mine when she spotted me hobbling about and heard the explanation was, "Well, baby, you're not as young as you used to be, you know."

I was enraged. There she goes, I thought, with that noxious phrase, "You're not as young as you used to be." Of course I'm not as young as I used to be! An eight year-old's not as young as he used to be at six, either. So the use of the phrase is, on the face of it, completely unwarranted. Yet with a few variations such as "I'm not as young as I used to be," or "He—she—or they are not as young as he—she—or they used to be," this particular phrase is one of the most prominent and most baleful stars in the dark firmament of word habits.

You may not share my feelings that your word habits are of great importance. But, as it happens, word habits are very important. They matter vitally in the process of staying young, and for very sound psychological reasons. You see, phrases that you make a practice of using in your conversation weigh in heavily on your psyche. Whatever your words, each time you utter them you hear them, and little by little, they make an ineradicable imprint on your unconscious. Those of you familiar with Emil Coue, the well-known pharmacist turned auto-hypnotist, are undoubtedly aware that this was the principle underlying his classic phrase which enjoyed such popularity some years ago. "Every day in every way I'm getting better and better." So what comes out of your mouth should command the same keen interest and sharp attention as what goes into it.

I know a man who's not quite 60 and yet he always says, at the slightest opportunity, "Well, I'm an old man." I'm sure if he heard anyone else refer to him in those terms he'd very much resent it. Because I don't for one minute think he really believes he's an old man. I notice that whenever he voices the words, they're invariably accompanied by an arch grin. My personal opinion is that the words serve as a handy excuse for him to slide out of whatever he doesn't particularly want to do. But be it an excuse or not, the repeated usage of the phrase is dangerous business. It can't help but deepen an unconscious acceptance of himself as old, and thus hasten his becoming, in Mr. Webster's words, "stale, shabby, belonging to the past."

Into this same category falls a whole assortment of hazardous word habits: "When you get to be my age," "I'm so bad at names lately," "I'm getting along, you know," "I can't do what I used to do," "I've got a mind like a sieve." These are a few of the more popular ones, all delivered usually in the same faintly funereal tone of voice.

And then there's the other old standby, "You can't teach an old dog new tricks." Under no conditions, let yourself get caught in the toils of that one. First off, you're labeling yourself an old dog, which is scarcely the most flattering appellation one could apply to oneself. Secondly, the phrase is such a hoary cliche, with such destructive overtones, that it's worthy only of being hustled along into desuetude.

And thirdly, and most importantly, it's a statement that happens to be wholly without accuracy. For in the research being currently conducted in the field of gerontology they have found that the ability to learn depreciates very little over the years if the will to learn is retained. It appears now you *can* teach an old dog new tricks. All the old dog has to decide is whether or not it wants to learn those tricks. So this word habit, outside of its other drawbacks, hasn't any validity.

Of course if I had my way, I'd arrange to have every one of these ruinous phrases stricken from the English language. I believe firmly that if we had no idea of how old we were—whether we were 40, or 50, or 70, or 90, we'd not only stay young longer, but we'd live a great many years more. And we'd be a great deal happier in those years. Actually, it's pointless to keep ticking off the years when you consider that length of life is not what matters at all. What is of any real consequence is its breadth.

So, except for statistical purposes, which present themselves relatively seldom, why not forget your age? At least give it a good try. You might miss out on a few birthday presents. But it would be well worth it, I think.

If you find, however, that you just can't swing it, if it makes you feel disoriented or perhaps deprived not to remember how old you are, then at least don't insist on broadcasting it to innocent bystanders. So many people, particularly when they get quite elderly, seem to be locked into this pernicious habit.

A man will announce proudly, "I'm 85, you know." You then feel called on to make a reply of some sort, usually a routinely polite one such as, "My, you certainly don't look 85." What else can you say? You can't very well come out with, "85? You know, you actually look 90," or "I'd have taken you for at least 94." It would serve him right, however, if you did. He should realize that most people are not even marginally interested in how old he is.

I assure you that people in general give your age no thought or interest whatsoever. NOR SHOULD YOU.

Nor should your children.

Sometimes children are the most flagrant offenders in this matter of word habits. "Mother," in a stern voice, "that's no way of carrying on at your time of life!" or, "Dad, at your age—really!"

Under no circumstances fling at your parents crushing words like these. First of all, what they choose to do at any age is none of your affair. Secondly, it they're willing to take the fifth amendment on their age you should be rooting for them, not chastising them.

Then, too, that particular word habit carries a double-edged sword. It not only says, "You're old! Act old!" when it's swung wickedly against the parent, but in later years it swings against you, the children, when it takes its place, as it assuredly will, in your own conversation, transformed, because of the passage of time, into the word habits, "Well, at my time of life," and "When you get to be my age..."

Consider running a check on yourself to see if any one of these word habits makes its home cozily in your vocabulary, perhaps without your even being aware of it. If any one of them does, throw it out now. And while you're at it, throw out every one of its sisters and its cousins and its aunts along with it.

You may not be able to accomplish this in one fell swoop when those habits have unwittingly been a part of your conversation over a long period of time. By very definition, word habits are phrases that have become solidly entrenched. But being thoroughly aware of the damage they're doing, I trust that you'll have no hesitation in making every possible effort to uproot them. If you'll take the trouble to do this, I assure you that you'll be pleasurably rewarded when you notice them, little by little, disappearing.

It's just possible for you to overlook one small word habit that's tucked in among all the others. You could miss it altogether becuase this one seems so innocuous. That deceptively innocuous one is the phrase, "I can't remember." I use the words "deceptively innocuous" advisedly because, in my opinion, the word habit, "I can't remember" is not in the least innocuous. What it's really saying is, "I'm unable to remember," which trails in its wake the traits of helplessness and inadequacy. And those two traits are particularly devastating concomitants of aging.

Unlike all the other destructive word habits, however, I'm not suggesting that you toss this one out. I only suggest that you toss out one word: the word 'can't.' And that you replace it with the word 'don't.'

This may seem quite a small change, even picayune perhaps, substituting "I don't remember" for "I can't remember" each time it comes up in your conversation. But just try it out and see how powerful is the difference. Unlike the words, "I can't remember" with their attendant feelings of inadequacy and helplessness, the phrase, "I don't remember" is a mere statement of fact, with no onus whatsoever attached to it. It does not damage your feeling of self-worth; it wreaks no havoc with any feeling of confidence you have in yourself. And, in the final analysis, it's your feeling about yourself that's the prime factor in helping you to stay young—or in pushing you to get old.

A little earlier in this chapter I recommended, you may recall, another prime factor in helping you to stay young. That was the recommendation that you forget your age. However, I also mentioned that there was one exception to this sweeping admonition: statistical purposes. When, for instance, you apply for a driver's license, or for a passport; when you fill out medical records; these are a few of the situations in which any attempt to ignore your age would be neither appropriate nor appreciated.

At times such as these, and at any other time when it's absolutely incumbent on you to face the fact of your age, there's a simple little habit that would be most profitable to incorporate into your thinking. Before your age, whatever it is, drop in the word 'only.' Instead of thinking, "Hey, I'm 40," or "I'm 60," or "I'm 74 now," think rather, "Hey, I'm only 40," or "I'm only 60," or "I'm only 75 now." Watch how magically it works—how it lifts your spirits a bit, straightens your shoulders a bit and puts a bit of a bounce in your stride.

A friend of mine, when I suggested this technique, dug in her heels and said, quite belligerently, "Why? Why kid yourself?"

Well, I don't consider it kidding yourself. I consider it a way of gaining a whole new perspective. All our lives we've been indoctrinated with the idea that our chronological age is set in granite. But don't you believe it! This one little word habit, seemingly so modest and unobtrusive, is in reality a Goliath, powerful enough to break up the granite and to knock years off your age.

16.

In my dictionary, which is a large, fat one, there are two complete, full-length columns devoted to the word 'play.' There may be other words in the dictionary to which equal space is allotted, but thus far I haven't come across them. I consider this of lovely significance. Because, in my opinion, as well as in Mr. Webster's apparently, play deserves to be given a lot of space.

Mr. Webster lists any number of variations in the use of the word play; the play of light, to play the flute, fountains playing, the play of wit, to play tricks, the amount of play in a steering wheel ... all entirely disparate applications of the word. But the sense of play to which I'm addressing myself is defined as "exercise or action intended for amusement or diversion, to frolic, to gambol." Even the words defining play seem to have a ring of airiness and jollity.

'Tis a pity that once we pass our teens this airiness and jollity are so often banished to the back burner. And this obtains with an alarmingly high degree of frequency as we come into our later years. That's the dangerous time. That's the time we're wide open to attack by "spectatoritis," an insidious disease of which the chief symptom is giving up being an active participant—sometimes all at once, sometimes gradually—and becoming an inert, passive onlooker. I might say, in passing, that the advent of television hasn't helped any. As a matter of fact, it's only made the disease more virulent and widespread.

Unfortunately, "spectatoritis" does not cease its ravages with just transforming its victims into passive onlookers. Those people afflicted with it become, quite commonly, in due process of time, prey to all manner of other diseases. This contention is borne out by a most highly respected medical authority, Dr. Robert Monroe.

Dr. Monroe, who conducted a geriatric clinic in Boston, the first such clinic in the world, found that exercise and play, such as simple games and dancing, has remarkably curative effects on patients suffering from some of those diseases: high blood pressure, arthritis, hypertensive heart disease, tremors and partial paralysis. Just play.

Of course the term 'just play' is a bit of a misnomer. When you juxtapose those two words, just and play, it sounds as though play were a negligible adjunct of living. Which it is unequivocally not. It's a real and essential element of life, fully as important, if not more so, in our adulthood as it was in our childhood. It's recreation that is literally re-creation. It re-creates almost every part of our entire body: it repairs our worn tissues, it energizes our glands, it quickens our hormones and enzymes, it increases the efficiency of our lungs, it strengthens our hearts and it speeds up our circulation. As the song goes, "Who could ask for anything more?"

And yet, there is something more. There's one admirable side effect of play: it helps to create a genial expression. And a genial expression is an enormous plus in at least making us look young. You're all aware, I'm sure, of that famous trademark of age: the bitterly curved down corners of the mouth. There's a story about a mortician who says very proudly, "In our mortuary work, if I may say so, we specialize in smiles." Well, by that time, if *I* may say so, it's a little late. Now, right now, is the time to specialize in smiles. And smiles, you'll find, pop out much more readily when you're involved in some sort of play.

Naturally the form of play will vary with the individual. I happen to think a very good form of play, one in which I was an enthusiastic participant for years and for which I am still gung-ho, is square dancing. Many of those who danced in my group were not chronologically young people. I remember one couple, a man and wife both somewhere in their seventies, who never missed a single one of our weekly sessions. And they told me that, in addition, they danced in their patio over the weekends with their children and grandchildren. Then, too, as did many of the others in our group, they attended every one of the square dance festivals that were scheduled anywhere in the area. Those festivals, incidentally, are not only great fun and dazzlingly colorful, but they offer a great opportunity to meet all sorts of new friends.

A variation that's also great fun is folk dancing. And it has all of the advantages offered by square dancing—plus one. Whereas in square dancing being part of a couple is a necessity, in folk dancing many of the dances are done in a circle and hence no partner is required.

You may run into a little difficulty locating a group in either of these categories that's convenient for you to attend. But most parks and many high schools house these groups. And if you should happen to draw a blank there, get in touch with your Department of Parks and Recreation. They'll be able to point you in the right direction. You'll find that once you've become part of a group, a vast assortment of other groups will open up before you. As a matter of fact, you'll find opening up before you a whole new world—of play.

Now dancing as a form of play might not have any appeal for you. Another form of play might. But make sure some form does.

Bicycling perhaps. Most of us rode bikes as children. So if you've strayed from it, get back on one and see how easily you pick up the knack again. It's like sex. No matter how long you've neglected it, you never forget how.

A friend of mine, a bicyclist, joined a group called the Los Angeles Wheelmen, whose praises he never ceases to sing. It seems they have long rides, short rides, sunny daytime rides, moonlit night rides, weekend excursions—something for everyone. Give them a call. If you don't live in the Los Angeles area, but you'd like to tie in with a group, you can drop a note to the national organization, the League of American Wheelmen, in Palatine, Illinois. They'll be more than happy to tell you if and where there's a branch in your city.

When I was in the offices of the Department of Parks and Recreation I picked up one of their brochures and I noticed, among the activities listed, Male Chorus and Mixed Chorus. I said to the woman in charge of the office, "You know, it's surprising that you get enough people with excellent voices to put together a chorus." She replied, "Oh, you don't have to have a wonderful voice to join our choruses. All you have to do is know how to open your mouth and stay on pitch." So if you can open your mouth and stay on pitch you might like to try out for a chorus. My husband, who loved to sing, said to me once, "You know, on those rare occasions when you're lucky enough to manage just one marvelous clear, bell-like tone, it's almost like having an orgasm!" So you see what a great form of play singing can be.

However, if you know for a certainty that you can't stay on pitch but you can open your mouth, look around for an amateur theatrical group to join. The first reaction from many of you will undoubtedly be a fast, "Oh, I couldn't possibly do that!" To which my reply is an even faster, "Oh yes, you could." You could certainly try it. Flora Burke did, with most agreeable results. Flora Burke is a jolly housewife from Prairie Village, Kansas, whose acting career took off unexpectedly at the age of 40 when her daughter's summer theatre couldn't find anyone else to play a character part.

"I heard the laughs," she says, "got good reviews and that was *it*." She carried on with acting in Kansas City regional theatre until, at age 58, she and her husband moved permanently to California. Now she has broken happily into show business in Hollywood, doing commercials and bit parts on television.

"It's a whole new fun life. And I love new experiences," said Mrs. Burke, whose most astonishing one allegedly occurred when she first caught sight of herself on the screen.

"To my great surprise, I saw a stout, middle-aged lady who was kind of a stranger to me," she laughed. "Inside, you see, I still feel 30, with a darling figure!"

Barbara Lemmons was another lady with no experience who just up and started acting when she was 43. Her children grown and her marriage on the rocks, she sold her home and moved to Los Angeles. She bought clothes, had pictures taken and within six months she was rehearsing in a play for Theatre Arts, later signing a contract with one of the leading commercial agencies in town.

"My friends mostly think I'm crazy," said Mrs. Lemmons. "But I've got the enthusiasm of 17 and the wisdom of 43. So how can you miss?"

Neither of these spunky ladies may turn out to be a Jane Fonda or a Jessica Tandy. But then they just may. It was Oliver Wendell Holmes who said that, "life was painting a picture, not doing a sum; you had to have a little faith that the picture would fill out as you go along." Which translates into, you never can tell what might result from what.

I know, as a small instance, that when I signed up for a six-week course in self-defense, I never expected it to turn out to be an exercise in play as well.

The purpose of the class was to teach men and women techniques that would be effective in foiling an attacker. We teamed up in pairs for the instruction, each of us alternating in the role of attacker and victim. When it was the turn of my friend, who attended the class with me, to play the role of attacker I took one look at her as she moved toward me and doubled over with laughter. The ferociousness on her face and the menace in her stance were so ludicrous I couldn't control my hilarity, let alone fend off her attack. And when it came my turn to play the attacker and I dashed at her fiercely, she was so convulsed with noisy runaway laughter that we had great difficulty in remaining on our feet, much less carrying out the directions of the instructor.

We're planning on taking the class again as we learned almost nothing from it. But they were the most rollicking, mirth-filled times either of us had enjoyed since we were small. I strongly advise you to enroll in one when you see it advertised. You'll learn much that's valuable. But even if you don't, it'll be worth every minute of your time and every penny of the money it costs you, if you have half the riotous, re-creating fun we did. Try it.

TRY IT, of course is my favorite phrase. It's another one that, like PLAN SOMETHING NEW, is worthy of being printed in huge letters on a bright placard and given a place of honor in your house. I guarantee it will net you some interesting results. Some of the things you try might not keep your interest, some might land you in jail, but I know one result that'll make it stunningly worthwhile—you'll stay young!

17.

One of the more deplorable and less apparent aspects of old age is that it's such a sly operator. As you know, it doesn't herald its appearance with a blare of trumpets or a roll of drums. And there's no such thing as an announcement such as "Well, that's it. That's the end of your youth and here I am—your old age." That's not how it functions at all. Most of the time it just gradually and unobtrusively does you in without your having the least idea that it's happening to you ... unless (I was never much of a believer in modesty) you're one of the lucky ones who's reading this book. In that case you certainly are aware by now of the major signals that point out to you when and if you've wandered off the youthful road and are trudging down the dusty gray path to aging.

However, along with the major signs posted on that road, it would behoove you to watch for some of the other little random signs that appear, those small but dangerously significant signs that are part and parcel of the routine of your everyday life, signs that might not even strike you as being worthy of your attention.

For instance, do you find that your dislike of inclement weather is on the rise? When it's raining, do you find yourself increasingly reluctant to venture forth? Do you find yourself saying, with a shudder, "Oh, I wouldn't go out in that rain?" If so, I trust you'll take notice of the fact that it doesn't occur to the young to be kept indoors by the rain. Or by the wind—or sleet or snow. Youth bundles up and strides out, facing the elements with relish. Or if not with actual relish, at least with indifference.

I remember one very rainy night having to cancel a date for

dinner at a friend's house. When I called, my friend's 12 year-old daughter answered the telephone.

"Honey," I said, "when your mother comes home will you please tell her not to expect me for dinner tonight."

"Oh, I'm sorry," she said. Then, "Is it because of the rain?"

"Oh no. It's a business thing that came up suddenly and I have to take care of it."

"I didn't think it was on account of the rain. Because I remember I heard you say once that if you break dates and won't go out when it's raining it's a sign you're getting to be an old lady. And I sure don't see any signs of you getting to be an old lady."

"Why thank you darling! And I'm fiercely flattered that you remember all the pearls that fall from my lips."

"Pearls?" she asked in a puzzled voice.

"All the things I say, I meant."

"Oh, not all," she said with the quick, lovely forthrightness of childhood. "I only remember the ones that are real cool."

I scribbled a mental note to myself to come out henceforth with nothing but real cool utterances. I hope I can make it.

But whether I manage it or not, please bear in mind the one real cool utterance I did manage, according to my young friend. If the rain is responsible for your cancelling your plans to attend any event that's interesting, that's diverting or that promises to be fun—even though this propensity starts occurring at 30 or 40 or 50—it's a resounding signal that you're already on the road to getting old.

Unless you're a cat. Then to balk at tackling the rain is not a sign of age. It's a sign of just being a cat. In that case, and only in that case, is it allowable.

There are a few other tell-tale signs of aging that some of you might be fascinated, perhaps even slightly amazed, to detect in yourselves.

I happened to be out shopping one afternoon with a long-time friend of mine who had just recently moved from Brentwood, a section of Los Angeles, over to the San Fernando Valley. Since we were both bridge players, I suggested that perhaps she might get up a game for that evening.

"Oh, I'd love to," she said. "But I couldn't get any of my friends to come, I'm sure. They don't even come to dinner any more when I invite them."

"Why not?"

"Well, they won't drive to the San Fernando Valley. They complain that it's a distance and the road is too winding—and it means driving home at night, back over the hills again..."

"Oh, it's not all that far."

"I know."

"And they don't come alone. Their husbands are with them, aren't they?"

"Oh sure. But the husbands won't do it either. They're the worst."

"How old are these people—103?"

She laughed. "As a matter of fact, they're only in their sixties, and early sixties at that. They're not old, really."

"Oh yes, they *are*. Really. They're *old*."

And they are, according to my lights. Really old. If you turn down invitations that would ordinarily be to your liking because there are distances involved—distances that are well within reason, YOU - ARE - OLD.

And if you grouse at any time that it's too much effort to take the car out of the garage when you've already put it away, YOU - ARE - OLD.

If, when there's no physical reason for it, you're making a habit of driving places less and less, you can be sure you're well down that heavily traveled road to getting old.

Even trying to break a small, relatively unimportant habit is difficult and takes doing, as I'm sure you've discovered and sometimes it takes drastic measures to accomplish it. I know for weeks after I moved my jewelry from one drawer into another, I was still pulling open the wrong drawer. Until finally I printed a little cardboard sign announcing NO JEWELRY HERE. I fastened it to the knob of the drawer which had held the jewelry originally, and that did the trick. Of course that's not what you'd call a drastic technique. But then neither was the habit a deeply ingrained one. It did, however, seem to call for some active, practical step to be taken. And I took it.

I took it because it helped put a quick end to my frustration.

But I also took it because it was a good method of staving off the onset of "spectatoritis." So long as you're actively participating—taking active steps to bring about what you want to happen, it's almost impossible to contract the dread disease, in any of its manifestations.

And the manifestations are legion. If you feel like playing bridge or gin rummy or backgammon and you make no move to arrange a game—if you sit and wait, hoping someone, somehow, will call you—that's one manifestation of the onset of "spectatoritis." And if no one does call you, do you take steps to locate a bridge club or a spot where they play backgammon and go there to play? Or do you wait for some sort of fun to drift into your life somehow?

If you're filled with a sense of outrage over an injustice that's being perpetrated do you make any kind of move, such as going door to door or stationing yourself on a corner with a petition? Or even send off a letter about it? Or do you perhaps sit back passively and hope it'll go away or be righted by someone else—somehow? If so, "spectatoritis" has almost certainly set in.

You know, when you wait for life to come along and happen *to* you, chances of it obliging are practically nil. Chances are overwhelming that nothing will happen to you at all. Except, of course, old age.

18.

I feel it's practically obligatory that any book dealing with any facet of aging should say a few words about retirement.

However, if I were permitted to say only one word on the subject, that word would be—DON'T. Whether you like it or not, it seems to be an immutable fact of life that man's essential function is to work. And when stripped of that function, he generally molders. Often he dies.

The head of personnel at North American Aviation told me that they became so concerned about the high rate of death among their employees only two years after they retired that the company instituted a policy of sending out a series of monthly letters, beginning when the employee reached the age of fifty, in an attempt to get them to start right then thinking about and preparing for that retirement. Some of the men, he said, had managed to survive retirement well but their numbers were very small compared with those who did not.

The answer to this prickly phenomenon is to be found in the inability of most humans of any age to tolerate idleness, to live with no purpose. John Steinbeck, the well-known writer, says, "It seems to me that when survival ceases to have a purpose, some great part of the life-force disappears. The retired man, having in himself no valid reason to be alive, soon ceases to be. He cannot combat diseases which could not kill during his active or productive life."

Even the American Medical Association's Committee on Aging had this to say about work: "For the majority of adults, young or old, work provides the primary outlet for capabilities. Whether they be housewife, laborer or business tycoon, all derive from their activity a sense of contribution, of self-worth and belonging.

This sense of purpose, or contribution to the human community, is as VITAL TO TOTAL HEALTH AS ARE ADEQUATE REST AND NUTRITION."

Personally, I lay the responsibility for our obligation to work squarely on the doorstep of the Old Man Upstairs. Way back, when He got so aggravated and chased Adam and Eve out of the garden of Eden, thundering at them that out of the "sweat of their faces would they eat their bread until they returned to the dust," right then and there the hapless pair had laid on them the necessity to toil throughout their entire lives. And, for better or for worse, we, their descendants, have had ever since the same necessity to toil.

So you see, when I exhort you never to retire, I'm backed up by two of the most venerable authorities: the American Medical Association and the Lord (not necessarily in that order.)

Naturally I realize that sometimes there is no choice in the matter. Retirement can be mandatory. Willy nilly, work is snatched from you. Even that, though, you can cope with successfully if you're armed with a proper understanding of the meaning of retirement.

Contrary to popular belief, retirement does not mean a time of rest after a lifetime of work. It doesn't mean a time of not-doing. It doesn't mean that one can cease being active and of genuine use in some way or another. No matter if it's your choice or if it's been foisted on you, what a successful retirment does mean is to enter a new occupation.

Not for money this time out. Although for those who choose, that may enter in. But whether money is involved or not, retirement should be thought of in terms of being a new job, with a chance to rectify old frustrations, and begin tromping through new lush pastures that can yield a bumper crop of personal satisfaction.

Before, however, embarking on a new job of any sort, a certain amount of thought is necessary, a certain amount of planning is called for, as is a certain amount of time spent acquainting oneself with the details of the terrain involved. And so with retirement. Since it is a new job, not only do you have to prepare for it, but you also have to work for it. With one major difference, you can handle things now all your own way. At last you no longer have a boss. Or, if you've been a boss, you no longer have any employees.

Don't, though, for one split second think this can't be a gigantic trauma for some of those who've been the boss. A man who sat at my table on a cruise I took recently was one of those who'd been a boss.

At breakfast he was always unhappily silent. At lunch he was sometimes surly—sometimes silent. At dinner he was usually quite drunk. But happily loquacious. During one of his spells of loquaciousness he told me that he'd retired just a year before and had sold his business, a large and lucrative one, I gathered, to his employees.

"Biggest damn mistake I ever made," he said, waving his martini glass in the air.

"Oh, honey," his wife said placatingly, "you know you don't mean that."

He swung around to face her. "The hell I don't!" Then he turned back to me and sorrowfully shaking his head, reiterated, "Biggest damn mistake I ever made." He gulped down the dregs of his martini and shouted, "Waiter—bring me another one of these. A double this time." He chuckled and leaning closer to me, said waggishly, "Wanna be sure I don't make 'nother big damn mistake."

Lou also had been a boss. He'd owned a chain of profitable men's clothing stores which I happened to know he'd sold for an exceedingly handsome sum. When I ran into him and his wife at the theatre one night I said to him genially, "Well, Lou, how do you like retirement?"

He said flatly, "It's murder."

"But you look well—tanned and fit ..."

He shrugged. "I'm playing golf almost every day. And goofing off generally." Then, with a shake of his head, "It's bad, Eve—bad."

His wife, with a tight, anxious smile, said, "Lou, why don't you tell Eve about the volunteer work you're doing at the Small Business Administration?"

"Oh," I said quickly, "that should be interesting."

"Well, it's not. The people who come in for help are so stupid you wouldn't believe them. And their ideas about the businesses they're planning to go into are so hopeless ... I won't be there for long, that's for sure."

I wanted very much to quote for Lou what Dr. George Perera, formerly professor of medicine and associate dean at the Columbia University College of Physicians and Surgeons, had to say about retirement. I knew, though, it would be of no use to him. Because in Lou's case, as in so many instances where a man has been the big-honcho-in-charge, power was, in his thinking, equated with happiness. And when the power slipped from his grasp, there was little that would suffice to take its place for him, which is truly, desperately unfortunate.

But Dr. Perera's words on retirement might, perchance, be of use to you. "No longer is one bound by boss, hierarchy, tradition, the careful ascent of promotional ladders, nor apprehension regarding duties, obligations, pay and pensions.

"One is free—free to say yea and nay, to work half as hard or twice as hard, or intermittently—free to moonlight or to quit if disenchanted. To be in this capacity provides an unusual degree of liberty. I would suggest a new description of this later period of life—the Elective Years."

In short, to Dr. Perera, retirement meant activity—but with complete freedom. Than which, I think, there are few things in the world that can be more delectable. He said not a word about money. And I would guess the reason for that was that because to him—certainly to me, from what I've personally observed—being the possessor of plenty of money has very little to do with a successful retirement.

In my opinion, probably the very finest bridge to successful retirement is an absorbing avocation which you've cultivated during your early or middle years. (Again—preparation.) And if you see to it that your avocational interest involves a cause big enough and worthy enough to grow into a major life interest, then you, for one, will never fall prey to the bleak, empty days and the sense of futility which is the saddest part of retirement for so many.

A friend of mine had no avocation in mind when she started attending meetings of Overweight Annonymous. She just desperately wanted to shed some 50 pounds. In a comparatively short time, not only had she dropped most of the weight but she had become so taken with the organization, both with its warm sociability and the really remarkable results it obtained, that she devoted practically all of her free time to it. Now, retired from her job, she's one of the top executives in O.A., working fully as hard and with a great deal more enthusiasm than she'd ever felt in her job. In one fell swoop, she acquired a lovely figure and, as it turned out, a lovely avocation.

Faye was another friend who, in spite of having quite an extensive social life, found that she had much too much empty time on her hands. So she volunteered to work at the university a couple of hours a week, teaching conversational English to foreign students. The students in her classes were so taken with her that they started waylaying her in the halls, shyly asking for her advice on personal problems. Usually she gave each of them her telephone number and encouraged them to call her at any time with any of their problems. She doesn't have much empty time any longer. Happily, she's almost as busy as Ann Landers with her telephone clientele. She also had to put aside time to answer the charming letters she receives from many of the students when they return to their homes in every part of the world. As I said earlier, life is "like painting a picture which fills out as you go along" and thus you can never foresee what will result from what.

Even being aware of this, however, an avocation may not be an answer for you at all. You may be one of the fortunate ones who enjoys your work so thoroughly that the idea of putting an end to it is a calamitous one. Well, who says you must put an end to it? Often, with a tad of ingenuity and a bit of creativity it's possible to continue your special skills as long as you choose.

My father, for instance, a very fine physician and surgeon, was one of those who enjoyed whole-heartedly what he did. Until one day, at the age of 62, he had a stroke. He was very difficult to deal with during his convalescence. For weeks, moody and silent, he just sat in his chair, staring out the window. He knew he would never be able to practice medicine again. And as it turned out, he was right. Although he regained his health generally, he never recovered the full use of his left arm.

But nothing daunted my father. Nothing had ever daunted him for long. He began leaving the house quite early each morning and when he came home in the late afternoon, he looked worn and tired. But he never uttered a word as to where he'd been.

Then one day he strode into the house, beaming, which, I must say, was a welcome 180 degree turnabout from his recent mood. He announced proudly that he was starting work three days a week in a free clinic. He couldn't wield a knife, of course, but he could take blood pressure, pulse readings, make diagnoses, prescribe medication ... "Lots of essential things they need done and that I can still do." Then, with a flash of his beautiful, boyish smile, "And you know, they seemed genuinely pleased to have me on their roster of physicians."

I was so moved by this man who had occupied such an eminent place in his profession and was now so filled with pride and pleasure to be doing what any young intern could handle that my eyes filled with tears.

"Hey—are you crying?" my father asked incredulously.

"No!" I snapped indignantly. "I've got something in my eye. I just wish I knew a good doctor who could take it out!"

He grinned at me as he handed me his handkerchief. "Well, why don't you drop in at the clinic tomorrow and I'll see if I can dredge one up."

He worked happily at that clinic three days a week almost until the day he died. And he never got old. He was never a victim of "outgrown usefulness" so why would he?

You might argue, of course, that for professional people it's a good deal simpler to continue working than it is for the ordinary layman.

Well, there was the man who sharpened my knives for years. He had a slender slit of a store where he sharpened knives, made keys, sold locks, etc. And then one day his rent was raised to such a prohibitive level that he decided to shut up shop. When he told me, I asked with concern, "What are you going to do, Joe?"

"Well, I've been thinking," he said. "And I don't think I want to open another shop. After all, I'm almost 70."

"But who's going to sharpen my knives!"

"Me."

"You are?"

"Like I said, I've been thinking a lot about it—and I figured out I've got this little pickup truck ... so instead of my customers coming to see me I'll just tootle around to them and sharpen their knives and make their keys—and whatever."

"What a great idea! I'll tell everybody I know."

"No, don't do that," he said hastily. "I'm only planning on working three, four days a week for a few hours."

"In that case, I'll tell almost everybody I know. Okay?"

He laughed and I could tell he was pleased. "Okay."

And he did just that. He had a thriving business three days a week—and a thriving social life to boot. Because I know of other people who did exactly what I did—invited him in for coffee and cake whenever his truck came around.

I don't happen to be personally acquainted with John and Constance Clemens. But I was struck by their story when I ran across it in the newspaper. It seems that John Clemens had been in sales for 30 years when, in his fifties, he was jolted with the news that his sales territory was being phased out and his job was coming to an end. The Clemenses had five children in high school and college who had to be considered so John was in no position to retire.

A good friend who was a chiropractor suggested that the practice of chiropractic might be a career option. For both John and Constance. After a lot of "soul-searching," as they put it, and because of their concern that another sales job at this point could lead to still another jolt a few years down the line when John Clemens' services would be even less marketable, they decided to pick up the option.

They sold their house and moved to Kansas City, where they had relatives, and both John and Constance enrolled in a chiropractic college. In the three years that followed (they completed the four year course in three) the Clemenses waited on tables in various restaurants to augment personal loans that kept them afloat. At the same time, John Clemens became so popular with the students that they elected him student body president.

Later in their school career, they obtained scholarships to help ease the financial burden and by the time you read this story, John and Constance Clemens will be part of a fine practice in Lake Havasu City, Arizona.

I have a strong hunch that there will be no further retirement for the Clemenses. John Clemens *had* his retirement, an enforced one, at age 55, and with thought and creativity and sweat and tears, he made sure there will never be another.

As you see, there are many kinds of retirement—and in each, many kinds of choices.

Yet, with the wondrous and variegated cluster of choices available, I still hear complaints from people about their "empty days." I must say it's difficult for me to have much patience with them. In my opinion empty days are in reality nothing but poor imagination. How can there be empty days in view of the existence of just the Sunday paper? With the list you can cull from its bountiful pages of books to read, lectures to attend, (many of them completely without cost) seminars to sign up for, art shows to visit, poetry readings to drop in on, movies to see, little theatres to frequent ... how can there be empty days?

Then, with all the involvement opportunities offered in those pages—the multiplicity of organizations eager for your services, be they skilled or unskilled, how could anyone possibly lament "empty days?"

If you find that there *are* "empty days" in the 365 allotted to you each year, then the sole reason is that you have chosen to make them so. And if, at whatever point in time your retirement rolls around, you find that it's not an unqualified success, that you're moldering in it, there's only one reason for that, too—YOU, baby.

19.

In the 13th Chapter of 1st Corinthians St. Paul says, "And though I have the gift of prophecy, and understand all mysteries, and all knowledge; and though I have all faith, so that I could remove mountains, and have not charity, I am nothing." He goes on through the entire chapter lauding the beauties of charity, which is, of course, synonymous with love. And he ends with the verse, "And now abideth faith, hope, charity, these three; but the greatest of these is charity."

Paul was one of the outstanding saints of the New Testament, and a profoundly religious man. So perhaps the scoffingly secular-minded among you might choose to discount his views on the importance of love. But let me quote for you from Sir James Crichton-Browne. Sir James was not a saint, but a British physician specializing in nervous and mental diseases. He was far removed from St. Paul in time and in almost every other possible respect, yet his views on the importance of love are strikingly similar. He said, "Those stay young the longest who love the most."

Even more emphatic in his views on the value of love is Dr. Smiley Blanton, one of whose books is entitled, *Love or Perish*. You can gather from that title the vital importance Dr. Blanton attached to love.

As widely disparate as were these three distinguished men—in background, nationality, training—it's obvious they were firmly united in one area; they all had strong feelings about the urgency of loving. Whether it be something or someone is not of real consequence. What is of consequence is that your capacity to feel keenly be burnished to a high lustre and that that lustre be sedulously maintained as long as you live.

I'm sure you've all met people—either older or younger—who are almost totally disinterested in everything. There seems to be nothing that serves to excite them or stir them deeply. And no matter what their age, they're old.

Goethe, the famed German writer, could never, by any stretch of the imagination, be lumped in this category. This was a man who remained involved with active love affairs throughout his entire life. When he was 75 he fell violently in love with a girl who rejected him and he wrote: "I'm lost in unconquerable desire. There is nothing left but flowing tears. Let them flow unceasingly, but they can never extinguish the fire that burns me."

Not bad, at any age. Certainly magnificent at 75! But Goethe was a deeply feeling man always and because of the power of his emotional life, his sexual feelings, too, not surprisingly, were deep and powerful.

And so, I will venture boldly to guess, was his sexual ability. For I think it would be accurate to say that those who retain longest their capacity to feel strongly not only stay young the longest but retain longest their power to make love.

I've heard men say—and women, too—after they've been badly clobbered in a romance or a marriage, "I'm not going to go through *that* any more! I'm never going to let myself get involved again." And they don't. They plaster a shield tightly about themselves and allow no deep commitment ever to pierce it.

In my opinion, that's tantamount to burning yourself on a red-hot stove, then hurling out the stove and resolving with fierce finality never to allow another one into your abode. A reaction such as that would be considered pretty rash—and exceedingly stupid, don't you think? And yet in the region of love, that same sort of behavior is accepted as entirely logical. Cut love off if you get badly burned and never let it through your door again! Logical? Not in the least. Nor intelligent. For the intelligent thing to do, seems to me, would be to come to the realization that you need, first of all, to learn how to handle love with more wisdom the next time around. And then, fortified with that usually hard-won wisdom, to stand ready to welcome love freely into your life once again.

Whenever love is the topic under discussion, the sort that springs to mind is, more often than not, sexual love. And yet there are countless other varieties—varieties of equal strength and of equal importance.

For one, there's the love of music—the fervent love we see so often in the faces of the men who conduct symphony orchestras. It's interesting that so many of these men seem to live exceptionally long and vigorous lives. I've speculated at length about that phenomenon and I've concluded that what's largely responsible for those long and vigorous lives is St. James Crichton-Browne's statement, "Those stay young the longest who love the most." There can be no doubt, with the love that shines so openly from their faces, that they move in the very forefront of those "who love the most."

Some of you may become equally alight with love at the sight of your children—or your grandchildren. And better yet, there are those of you who burn with an abiding love for your fellowman, manifested in liberality with your time—or your money. Or perhaps, and preferably, with both.

Then, for those of you who, in spite of the generally irreligious climate of the times, hold stoutly to the faith of your forefathers, there is that wonderful outlet, the love of God. I'm not talking about it's Sunday-and-time-to-get-down-on-your-knees love of God. I'm referring to the love that is evidenced by everyday generosity, kindness, understanding, thoughtfulness. I remember a nursing home operator telling me that in all her years of experience with men and women in the various rest homes she'd managed, the only ones she'd found who were not totally involved with themselves, who were cheerful, and undemanding with their children when they came to visit, were men and women who had some sort of spiritual faith.

The ways are many—and they're simple, easy ways—that enable you to keep open the door of your heart ... That letter you're always meaning to write and just don't somehow. Why not write it? That's caring. That's love.

And the clipping you cut out because you knew it would be of special interest to a friend and then misplaced or never got around to giving. Find it! See to it that he or she gets it. That's kindness and it's loving.

How about that small gesture of thanks when a friend has recommended to you a doctor or a lawyer or a plumber and you've been gratified with the end result. Or even if it hasn't panned out successfully, how about telephoning and giving your friend a rundown, instead of letting the entire episode slide, as it so often does, into an abyss of silence. Or what of the recipe someone has taken the trouble to write down for you? Did you drop them a little note or phone them and let them know how it came out? That's thoughtfulness and it's loving.

Too, be generous with your compliments. Strew them around with a lavish hand. I turned to a man in a store the other day—a complete stranger—and said to him, "I hope you won't mind but I just have to tell you what perfectly beautiful, luxuriant hair you have."

He was somewhat taken aback. Then belatedly, a little stiffly, he said, "Thank you." But as he walked out, I noticed that he ran a hand over his beautiful, luxuriant hair and there was a small smile of pleasure flickering at the corners of his mouth.

I do things like this because I find it great fun to make people feel good. But I also do them for a purely selfish reason. Because I remember well Dr. Blanton's warning, "Love or Perish." I remember what St. Paul said, "The greatest of these is love." And I remember with special vividness the words of Sir James Crichton-Browne, "Those stay young the longest who love the most." And me—I'm determined to stay young the very longest. As I said at the opening of this book, I have no intention of ever becoming, as Sean O'Casey phrased it, "a misery to myself and a damned nuisance to others." And I'm willing to do whatever it costs to avoid that.

There's an old Chinese proverb that reads, "We cannot prevent the birds of sorrow from flying over our heads, but we *can* keep them from nesting in our hair." And I like to paraphrase it as follows: "We cannot prevent the calendar years from piling up on us but we *can* keep them from making us old!"

Usually books have a foreword. But I've rarely set eyes on an aftword. Well, in this book there's an aftword—and, with my very best wishes, here it is:

Lord, thou knowest I am growing older

Keep me from becoming talkative and possessed with the idea that I must express myself on every goddam subject.

Release me from the craving to straighten out everyone's affairs.

Keep my mind free from the recital of endless detail. Give me wings to get to the point.

Seal my lips when I am inclined to tell of my aches and pains. They are increasing with the years and my love to speak of them grows sweeter as time goes by.

Teach me the glorious lesson that occasionally I may be wrong. Make me interested but not nosey—helpful but not bossy.

With my vast store of wisdom and experience it does seem a pity not to use it all. But thou knowest, dear Lord, that I want a few friends at the end. Amen.